A GATEWAY TO THE KABBALAH

A Spiritual Journey through History

Rabbi Eugene A. Wernick

United Synagogue of Conservative Judaism
NEW YORK

ISBN: 978-0-8381-0001-1

COVER ART AND SEFIRAH DIAGRAM BY YOSSI TOCKER

DESIGN AND COMPOSITION BY MILES B. COHEN

PRINTED IN THE UNITED STATES OF AMERICA

The publication of
A Gateway to the Kabbalah
has been made possible
through the generosity of
Sheila Reinstein

in honor of her granddaughters,
Hannah Chan Beth Widmayer
and
Lillie Yu Anne Widmayer,
becoming B'not Mitzvah

and in memory of her daughter,
Shari Sue Reinstein Widmayer.

CONTENTS

Preface

Over fifty years ago, I sat in the Unterberg Auditorium of the Jewish Theological Seminary when Professor Saul Lieberman, foremost authority on Rabbinic studies of his day, introduced a lecture by Professor Gershom Scholem. In a witty way, but nonetheless disparaging, Lieberman introduced his friend Scholem as being an authority on a subject of lesser value than Lieberman's. In this, Lieberman was continuing the tradition of the Seminary, which believed itself to be the heir of the Jewish Theological Seminary of Breslau, Germany, the foremost institution of *Wissenschaft des Judentums* (the science of Judaism). The German Jewish scholarship of the nineteenth and twentieth centuries discounted and ignored the contribution of Jewish mysticism to the development of Jewish religion and civilization.

Being a curious student, I was attracted to this semi-forbidden discipline, and I began to read anything that Scholem had written. This began a long process of on-and-off study during a long and difficult personal life, while maintaining a rabbinical career and active service in community affairs.

As a teacher of Talmud Honors in a Solomon Schechter Day School, I was determined to introduce a course in Mysticism to expose my students to that hidden subject whose influence had made a much bigger impact on Jewish life than was readily acknowledged. Out of devotion to Scholem and the impact he had made on Jewish studies, I selected as the text for the course his *Major Trends in Jewish Mysticism*, supplemented by readings in the sources and works by more recent scholars. I prepared guide questions for each chapter and hoped that my brilliant students would be able to master the material. I found to my dismay that beyond the readings in Hebrew and Aramaic, it was the language of scholarship that sent my students too often to the English dictionary. I determined that I would attempt to present an easy access to the main ideas of this subject for a lay readership; this book is the result of that effort. The more one teaches the more one learns. "From all my teachers I have gained insight" (Pirkei Avot 4:1). I dedicate this book to my students whose love I cherish.

For those who follow the spiritual path know full well:
If you do not seek, you will not find.
If you seek, you will not find until you are found.

Introduction

The Dalai Lama once asked what the key was to the survival of the Jewish people through their long years of exile.[1] Throughout the ages, exile, persecution and massacres have followed the Jews wherever they have dwelled. Yet despite the "slings and arrows of outrageous fortune," the Jews not only have survived but have risen to great heights in practically every field of human endeavor. Is it nature or nurture or something else that fuels the Jewish will to survive despite the forces that have relegated the great empires of the past to the dustbin of history?

The answer may well be found in the sense of mission that was cultivated in the most ancient documents of their faith. The Bible states "that man does not live by bread alone but on all that comes from the mouth of the Lord" (Deuteronomy 8:3). If one should then see that it is only the word of God that is important, then the word that has been transmitted to you and your people is a most precious gift. The story of the Exodus from Egypt is one of the most memorable events that Jewish children experience as they participate, through the Haggadah, in the re-enacting of the event every year at the Seder (Passover meal). That same book of the Bible declares to the Jewish people:

> You have seen what I did to the Egyptians; and I carried you on eagles' wings and brought you to Me. And now if you will listen to My voice and keep My treaty and you will be special to Me from all other peoples because the world is Mine. You will be to Me a kingdom of priests and a holy nation." (Exodus 19:4–5)

Throughout the centuries, Jews have nurtured an intimate relationship with God. There are no intermediaries. Even Moses himself is mentioned hardly at all in the telling of the Passover.

In a past generation, during a prayer service one might hear a sigh coming from a Jew from Eastern Europe: *Oy Tate Ziesenyu* (O dear sweet Father). As the Jewish people suffered exiles and returns, persecutions and degradations, a thinking person could well ask where is that "dear sweet Father" who promised so much and seems to have given so little.

Rather than reject the promise and the traditions, those of faith chose to try to pierce the veil of mystery that seemed to hide that "sweet Father" from His people. The result was the rise of mystical speculation which reinforced the beliefs and concepts of the past and provided a new reality to those who chose its path. That faith in the path and in the goal gave those who held fast to it the strength to overcome all obstacles that any human force could hurl against them.

In the nineteenth century, under the influence of assimilation, German Jewish scholarship (that of *Wissenschaft des Judentums*, or the science of Judaism) rejected the irrational, indecorous, and unregimented religious life that they saw as the hallmark of their embarrassing brethren from the east. The result was to transform western Jewry and its attitudes about prayer and mysticism.[2]

Only after the Holocaust did the scholarship of Gershom Scholem and the philosophies of Martin Buber and Abraham Joshua Heschel draw western Jewry back to the roots of its strength. The infiltration of Buddhism and other eastern religions into the western cultural mix and the flowering of the Hippie subculture also made spiritual exploration attractive once again.[3]

Kabbalah (tradition) is the name used for Jewish mysticism, although properly speaking it applies only to the latest form thereof. The mystics that could properly be called Kabbalists emerged in southern France and Spain in the 1200s.[4]

The lure of a hidden spiritual world that surrounds us in a different dimension of space or time is the strongest attraction to the study of the Kabbalah. For centuries, students of Kabbalah have drawn spiritual sustenance from its wellsprings. My purpose in this book is to give you accessible insight and a guided path to the origins and practice of Kabbalah.

NOTES

1. Rodger Kamenetz, *The Jew in the Lotus* (San Francisco: HarperOne, 1994), 2.

2. *B'rikh sh'mei d'marei almah* is a prayer that has its source in the Zohar and which is recited at the ark before removing the Torah. In the services at the Jewish Theological Seminary in New York, there was a time when the prayer was not said because it had not been said in the Jewish Theological Seminary of Breslau!

3. Kamenetz, op. cit.

4. Gershom Scholem, *Major Trends in Jewish Mysticism* (New York: Schocken Books, 1961), 119 f.

For the Reader

Translations of Biblical Texts

All translations from the Hebrew Bible are taken from The Holy Scriptures: According to the Masoretic Text, edited by Max Margolis (Philadelphia: The Jewish Publication Society, 1917). I have modified the language to eliminate where possible forms of speech that are no longer in use.

Transliterations

The transliteration to English from Hebrew—or from any other non-Latin alphabet—is a subjective undertaking. The transliterations and respellings in *A Gateway to the Kabbalah* may seem inconsistent. However, a conscious decision was made to reflect source materials, commonly accepted forms for certain words, and other historical or traditional criteria rather than to overlay a rigid format.

Words of Thanks and Gratitude

I would like to thank my editors: Dorrie Berkowitz, whose kind and gentle advice led me through the pathways of book publishing; Jacquelyn Julie, my one-time student became my teacher as she artfully did the copyediting, a longer process than I could have ever imagined.

My gratitude and praise to that which guides this Universe for blessing me with my wife, Irene Gilbert, and all of our children and grandchildren. After a life filled with sufficient sorrows, I have been granted the blessings of peace and consolation and the joy of not only my children and grandchildren but the many, many students to whom I am bound by bonds of love.

מלכות

1 Occult Origins
Exile and Return

Sanctus, Sanctus, Sanctus, Dominus Deus Sabaoth.
Pleni sunt caeli et terra gloria tua.

The choir of Saint Catherine of Siena chanted the Latin words, echoing the cantor's Hebrew:

Kadosh, Kadosh, Kadosh, Adonai Tzvaot.
Melo kol haaretz kevodo.

Holy, Holy, Holy is the Lord of Hosts.
The whole earth is full of His glory.[1]

The glory of God permeated the sanctuary of Temple Beth El in Allentown, Pennsylvania, that night. Pope John Paul II had encouraged Catholics and Jews to share the gifts of faith, so Bishop Thomas Welsh and I planned this Service of Reconciliation to unify our congregations. Across the centuries since "the parting of the ways," when Christianity and Judaism split, prejudice and persecution separated the two religions that sang these same verses in different tongues. Yet at that moment the words of the prophet, found in the sixth chapter of Isaiah, united all that sang his anthem. The common goal of both journeys toward that Jerusalem on high obliterated the misunderstandings of the past. I turned to my new friend and smiled.

The prophets of Israel were pioneers of faith who taught the peoples of the world the exaltation of Divine communion. Isaiah is overcome by a force that fills him with awe and submission. Chapter six recounts his dream of standing in the Temple of Solomon in Jerusalem. He is not looking for God. God comes to him, and Isaiah feels obliged to execute the will of the power that is to direct his destiny. I refer to what is described by prophets in the Hebrew Bible as the primary religious experience.

This experience is received by Moses at the burning bush, Ezekiel at the river Chebar, and Jacob at Beth El, where he exclaims awakening from his dream: "For sure, God was in this place and I did not know it."[2] In the biblical story, Jacob is fleeing his firstborn brother, whom he tricked out of birthright and blessing. About to leave the country of his birth, he fears for his life on the road to his uncle.[3] Asleep for the last time on his home ground, Jacob's anxiety is answered by a dream of angels ascending and descending a ladder to Heaven and the voice of God assuring him of protection. Perhaps this prophecy inspired the founders of my own Temple Beth El, as they planted roots in a foreign land they hoped to be their new home and established a synagogue that would be their *beth El* ("house of God").

For everyone who has wished, now wishes, or will wish for the spiritual experience that moved the prophets of old, the path is not a simple one. Mysticism is the attempt by its devotees to experience God or gods in an intimate way that mystics have likened to the sexual union of lovers. The mystic seeks the experience that found the prophet unawares.[4] It is what I call the secondary religious experience, as it is not a spontaneous meeting with the Divine. This spiritual quest is not restricted to any particular faith and is achieved through physical activity such as prayer, meditation, fasting, and listening to music.[5]

One constant theme that runs throughout the ages is the tension between normative religious authority, belief, and practice and the defiant flight of mystics. In the Bible we meet a strange group known as the *Bnei HaNeviim* (members of a prophetic fraternity). They are wandering ecstatics who, in a possession-like state, engage in wild actions such as stripping and lying on the ground for prolonged periods. The texts include nonsense syllables, hinting that they speak in tongues. Apparently others unconnected to the group fall under its spell, as is related of King Saul, who, in his murderous pursuit of David, catches the spirit of adjacent prophesiers and lies naked all day and night, enabling David's escape.[6]

The prophets and prophetic fraternities were part and parcel of the First Temple Israelite religious landscape. Functionaries of the faith were not limited to certain tasks. Samuel, as also told of Moses, was a priest who offered sacrifice as well as a prophet who saw the future and transmitted the will of God. Samuel supported the Bnei HaNeviim and they served him as a retinue.[7]

The Hebrew Bible is more than a spiritual record and guide; it chronicles the historical vicissitudes of ancient peoples. A great watershed in Israelite history was the exiles of the northern kingdom, Samaria, in 722 BCE and the southern kingdom, Judea, in 597 and 586 BCE. The Israelite kingdoms, caught between the forces of Egypt and the Mesopotamian empires, chose alliances with Egypt against the warnings of the prophets, resulting in the Babylonians and Assyrians coming down like wolves on the fold. The Mesopotamian invaders demolished the main sanctuaries of Samaria and Judea. Given the importance of the Temple in Jerusalem, its destruction was a heavy blow to the religious cult bound to it. The Babylonian and Assyrian empires exiled large portions of the upper classes to the vicinities of their capitals to contain revolt in the conquered lands.

The Bnei HaNeviim disbanded, and the priests had no sacrifices to offer on foreign soil. Instead, the two outstanding prophets of the exile, Ezekiel and the Second Isaiah,[8] shaped the belief that once Divine punishment was accomplished for the sin of being unfaithful to the covenant, the exiles would be restored to their native land.[9] By 540 BCE, Cyrus the Great, King of the Medes and Persians, conquered the Babylonian empire, freed the captive Jews, encouraged them to reestablish their religion in their homeland—as prophesied—and financed the rebuilding of their Temple. The Persian policy of permitting exiles to return to their native lands represented an enlightened view that was sure to cement loyalty in those populations.

A new type of secular and religious authority arose in Nehemiah (c. 450 BCE), an official of the Gentile government, and Ezra the Scribe (c. 458 BCE), a prototype of what later was to become Jewish lay leadership. Nehemiah and Ezra were servants of the Persian king. Functioning as a provincial governor in the former southern kingdom, Nehemiah rebuilt the walls of Jerusalem, banished foreign wives, and ensured the people would support the Temple cult. Ezra collaborated with Nehemiah to dissolve mixed marriages and arranged public Torah readings at the Water Gate in Jerusalem, where the Levites interpreted the words for the assembly.[10] The prophet Malachi, who was active before Ezra, casts the priest as the lone explicator of the Law of Moses.[11] The loss of the Temple must have debased the power of the priesthood sufficiently to empower non-priests, such as the Levites at first and then the ordinary laity, to attempt the interpretation of the Torah.

After the destruction of the first Temple, the prophetic occurrence waned. Direct communication with God became increasingly rare and was replaced by intermediaries such as angels. The first chapter of Zachariah is a prophesy by dream, in which an angel conveys God's will for the Holy Temple to be rebuilt in Jerusalem:

> **12**Then the angel of the Lord spoke and said: O Lord of hosts, how long will You not have mercy on Jerusalem and on the cities of Judah, against which You have had indignation these threescore and ten years? **13**And the Lord answered the angel that spoke with me with good words, even comforting words— **14**so the angel that spoke with me said unto me. . . . **16**Therefore thus says the Lord: I return to Jerusalem with mercy: My house shall be built in it, says the Lord of hosts, and a line shall be stretched forth over Jerusalem.**17**Again, proclaim, saying: Thus says the Lord of hosts: My cities shall again overflow with prosperity; and the Lord shall yet comfort Zion, and shall yet choose Jerusalem.[12]

The three speakers—the Lord, the angel of the Lord, and the prophet-narrator—are indirect interlocutors. Zachariah does not receive his prophesy from the Divine but is witness to God's "good . . . comforting words." The angel then relays His message, providing the prophetic script. The seventy years of indignation probably count from the time the first Temple was destroyed in 587 BCE until the second Temple was consecrated in 516 BCE. Zachariah was active in the first part of the Second Temple period, which lasted until the destruction of the second Temple in 70 CE.

For the first time, whether in Israel or other lands of the Persian Empire, Jews were confronted with more sophisticated forms of foreign religion. The Persian belief in what became Zoroastrianism rationalized the existence of evil in the world; a lesser god challenged the creating god of light, wisdom, and truth. Contrary to this belief in the duality of universal power, the Second Isaiah prophesies on behalf of the one Abrahamic God: "Fashioner of light and creator of darkness; maker of peace and creator of evil; I am the Lord maker of all these."[13] The rabbis did not wish to refer to the omnibenevolent God as the "creator of evil," yet they believed in God's omnipotence, so how could evil enter the world if it was not in some way created by God? Their solution is found in the first morning blessing before the Shema prayer (Deuteronomy 6:4). The rabbis transformed the prophet's words to read: "Praised are You Lord our God King of the World, Fashioner of light and creator of darkness; maker of peace and creator of *all*" (emphasis added). The later kabbalists would not find this solution satisfying, and the problem of evil is still a conundrum that confronts the faithful.

The existence of evil is a principal paradox for any monotheistic religion. The story of the fall of Adam in Genesis is one attempt at an explanation. But reward for the righteous and punishment for evildoers could no longer be rectified with what happened to people during their lifetimes. Why did the wicked prosper and the righteous suffer? It became a common religious paradigm to justify worldly inequity with posthumous Divine retribution. During the Persian period Jews accepted two competing afterlife models: bodily resurrection or Heaven and Hell. It is quite possible that the latter concept was influenced by Greek thought.

Prior to the Persian period, the Israelites had enough knowledge of the early Greeks to track their descendence from Noah. Euripides' Alcestis of 438 BCE refers to "Thracian tablets which tuneful Orpheus carved out" just as Moses on Sinai, evidencing crossover between the Orphic and Jewish traditions.[14] The Bible references Ionia, the ancient Greek settlement of western Anatolia,[15] where a student of Aristotle recorded a meeting between his master and Jews.[16]

The Greek settlement of Ionia was under the domination of the Persian Empire, but the city-states of the Greek mainland wavered in their support of imperial interests. In response to an Ionian revolt, the Persian King Darius invaded Greece and was defeated at Marathon in 490 BCE. His son suffered defeat at Thermopylae and Salamis ten years later. Although Persians fought the Greeks unsuccessfully, there always were Greeks in the service of Persian kings.[17] Trade between Greece and the Empire most probably brought not only the exchange of goods but also ideas. Ripe for Hellenic and imperial influence, Israel faces west to the Mediterranean and east to Mesopotamia.

Championing their progressive policies, the Persians, speaking an Indo-European language but ruling an empire inhabited mainly by Semitic speakers, did a strange thing for then and any time. They made Aramaic, a Semitic language cognate to Hebrew, the chief language of their empire. The Jews began to use Aramaic in their daily discourse and changed their writing system to a variant of the Aramaic alphabet. The Second Temple period was one of religious creativity and textual prolificacy in the newly adopted script.

While contemporary scholarship has achieved a great deal in understanding the texts of this period, there is much to be learned. In the startling revelation of the Dead Sea Scrolls, we became acquainted with a literature hitherto unknown. Scholars still are debating to which sect of Jews the Dead Sea Scrolls belonged. The literature that was studied up to our present time is contained in two separate collections known as Apocrypha and Pseudepigrapha.[18]

These two collections were a group of writings that did not make the cut into what was to be called the Bible or Holy Scripture. The Jewish scholars of the Second Temple period organized the Hebrew Bible into a tripartite division in a descending order of holiness, the Torah ("Teaching") being the first five books from Genesis to Deuteronomy. Then came the Prophets followed by those books known as the Sacred Writings. As late as the second century CE, decisions were being made as to which texts to include or exclude from these Sacred Writings. So we can just imagine how many books were deemed unfit to be preserved.

The Persian period came to an end with the conquest of that empire by Alexander of Macedon in 331 BCE. After Alexander's death his empire was divided among his generals, and Israel was seized by the Ptolemaic Kingdom of Egypt and then the Seleucid Empire of the east. A growing diaspora of Jews spread throughout the Mediterranean world, with its center in the intellectual capital of the Hellenistic world: Alexandria of Egypt. Jews now were exposed to the religions and magic of both Asia and Greece.[19] It was during this period of Greek ascendency throughout the eastern Mediterranean that the books of the Apocrypha and Pseudepigrapha were composed. This literature revealed a desire to become familiar with the scenery of Heaven and lay the groundwork for the major themes of what was to follow.

An important work, the book of Enoch, is preserved only in an Ethiopic translation of what had to be an original Hebrew or Aramaic text, which probably was translated first into Greek. This sequence shows us that those who later determined what was acceptable were not too keen on preserving this literature.[20] Enoch, according to the fifth chapter of Genesis, does not die but is transported by God to a heavenly abode:

> 21And Enoch lived sixty and five years, and begot Methuselah. 22And Enoch walked with God after he begot Methuselah three hundred years, and begot sons and daughters. 23And all the days of Enoch were three hundred sixty and five years. 24And Enoch walked with God, and he was not; for God took him.

In chapter fourteen of Enoch, the prophet delivers a Divine ruling condemning the "eternal Watchers . . . the children of Heaven" to be bound to the world, relating a vision he has of being swept up to a heavenly house with marble walls and tessellated floors to receive God's message:[21]

> 8And the vision was shown to me thus: Behold, in the vision clouds invited me and a mist summoned me, and the course of the stars and the lightnings sped and hastened me, and the winds in 9the vision caused me to fly and lifted me upward, and bore me into Heaven. And I went in till I drew nigh to a wall, which was built of crystals and surrounded by tongues of fire: and it began to affright 10me. And I went into the tongues of fire and drew nigh to a large house, which was built of crystals: and the walls of the house were like a tessellated floor of crystals, and its groundwork was 11of crystal. Its ceiling was like the path of the stars and the lightnings, and between them were 12fiery cherubim, and their Heaven was [clear as] water. A flaming fire surrounded the walls, and its 13portals blazed with fire. And I entered into that house, and it was hot as fire and cold as ice.

The themes of books such as Enoch, with the transport to Heaven and the description thereof, probably were the reasons for their neglect by rabbinic officials. As we shall see later, Rabbi Yehudah HaNasi, the editor of the Mishnah (the third-century CE guide to Jewish practice and belief) severely limited mystical speculation only to those who could be trusted with it.[22]

The Seleucid Empire under its king, Antiochus IV Epiphanes, taking advantage of a civil war between Hellenized Jews who were assimilating to Greek ways and traditionalists determined to preserve Jewish religion and custom, tried to impose the cult of Zeus and thus sparked a rebellion. In the midst of that war, which was to produce the holiday of Hanukkah, we have one of the earliest tracts of propaganda in the book of Daniel.[23]

Just as in the book of Enoch, there are "watchers" and "holy ones" who determine the fate of future events.[24] In Daniel we are introduced to a host of heavenly angels who serve God; Michael and Gabriel are mentioned by name. The author of the book tries to bolster the spirits of those fighting Antiochus by telling the story of young Jewish men who, under the most difficult circumstances in Babylonia, held fast to their faith and their God rescued them. As in the book of Zachariah, we have night visions in chapter seven:

> 1In the first year of Belshazzar king of Babylon Daniel had a dream and visions of his head upon his bed; then he wrote the dream and told the sum of the matters. 2Daniel spoke and said: I saw in my vision by night, and, behold, the four winds of the Heaven broke forth upon the great sea. 3And four great beasts came up from the sea, diverse one from another. 4The first was like a lion, and had eagle's wings; I beheld till the wings thereof were plucked off, and it was lifted up from the earth, and made stand upon two feet as a man, and a man's heart was given to it.

The point is that we have a transition from an interest in God's worldly workings to His heavenly activities. As in the Greek and later Roman descriptions of trips to Hades, so too in the Jewish world we have descriptions of trips to Heaven. How much of this reflects cross-cultural connection is a matter of scholarly conjecture.[25]

NOTES

1. Isa. 6. All biblical translations are from The Holy Scriptures: According to the Masoretic Text, ed. Max Margolis (Philadelphia: The Jewish Publication Society, 1917), but I have modified the English to eliminate antiquated forms of speech wherever possible.
2. Gen. 28:16.
3. Could this story be the inspiration for the account of Saul's conversion to Paul, another roadside revelation? See Acts 9:1–31, 22:1–22, 26:9–24.
4. See "*Yedid Nefesh*" (ascribed to Rabbi Elazar ben Moshe Azikri) *Mesorah Siddur Yitzchak Yair HaShalem, Nusach Ashkenaz* (Brooklyn: Mesorah Publications, Ltd., 1994) pocket-size edition, 260. See also John of the Cross, *A Spiritual Canticle of the Soul and the Bridegroom Christ* (London: limovia.net, 2012), ePub edition. If John was of converso background, he could have been influenced by *Yedid Nefesh* as well as by Rabbi Akiva's interpretation of Song of Sol.
5. 1 Sam. 10:5–12.
6. Ibid., 19:23–24.
7. See "Prophets and Prophecy," *Jewish Encyclopedia,* http://www.jewishencyclopedia.com/articles/12389-prophets-and-prophecy.
8. Bernhard W. Anderson, *Understanding the Old Testament* (Upper Saddle River: Prentice Hall, 1957) abridged fourth edition, 421 ff. Second Isaiah is the name given to the supposed author of Isa. 40–66 because of the clear departure in style from the preceding chapters. Isaiah functioned c. 135 BCE and Second Isaiah functioned c. 500 BCE.
9. Especially Ezek. 37.
10. See Ezra, Neh., and Anderson, op. cit., 469–479.
11. Mal. 2:6–7.
12. Zech. 2.

13. Isa. 45:7.

14. W.K.C. Guthrie, *Orpheus and Greek Religion* (Princeton: Princeton University Press, 1993).

15. Gen. 10:1.

16. Flavius Josephus *Contra Apionem* I, xxii. See "Aristotle in Jewish Legend," *Jewish Encyclopedia,* http://www.jewishencyclopedia.com/articles/1774-aristotle-in-jewish-legend.

17. See Xenophon *Anabasis.*

18. R. H. Charles, ed. *The Apocrypha and Pseudepigrapha of the Old Testament,* vols. I and II (Oxford: Oxford at the Clarendon Press, 1966). For a modern critical evaluation, see Otto Eissfeldt, *The Old Testament,* trans. Peter R. Ackroyd (New York: Harper & Row Publishers, 1966).

19. See E. R. Goodenough, *Jewish Symbols in the Greco-Roman Period* (Princeton: Princeton University Press, 1953–1968) Bollingen Series 37, and Gershom Scholem, *Jewish Gnosticism, Merkabah Mysticism, and the Talmudic Tradition* (New York: The Jewish Theological Seminary of America: 1960).

20. Charles, op. cit., II, 186 f.

21. The description of *pardes* ("paradise") in the Talmudic account of the ascent of Rabbi Akiva and his companions is too similar to be coincidental; see Hagigah 14b.

22. Mishnah Hagigah 2:1.

23. H. Louis Ginsberg, *Studies in Daniel* (New York: The Jewish Theological Seminary of America, 1948). Ginsberg maintains that a former legendary account of a hero by the name of Daniel was reworked during the persecution of Antiochus IV Epiphanes. See Anderson, op. cit., 558 f.

24. Dan. 4:14.

25. The most widely circulated tales of trips to Hades in the Greco-Roman world are the myth of Orpheus rescuing Eurydice, Odysseus in *The Odyssey* of Homer, and Aeneas speaking with his father in *The Aeneid* of Virgil. In earlier history we have the Sumerian tales of the descent of Inaana rescuing Dumuzi and Gilgamesh meeting Utapishtim. One of the questions that must be asked of comparative studies is does similar material imply borrowing or is it possible for independent development to produce analogous results? See M. L. West, *The East Face of Helicon: West Asiatic Elements in Greek Poetry and Myth* (Oxford: Oxford University Press, 1997) 402 f.

2 The Greco-Roman World

The Mishnah, the Maccabees, and Merkavah Mysticism

The Hasidim ("pious ones"), venerating the written and oral traditions of their ancestors, opposed the Hellenists, their fellow Jews who assimilated to the Greek lifestyle of the Seleucid Empire. But the Hasidim alone never would have defeated the Hellenists, as these assimilationists were backed by imperial power. In 165 BCE the Hasmoneans (Maccabees), championing the ways of the faithful but representing a more warlike and nationalist perspective, won the restoration of the Temple service commemorated by Hanukkah, the Jewish Festival of Lights. Simon, the last standing brother of the sons of Mattathias, was proclaimed high priest and leader of the Jewish people in approximately 140 BCE.[1]

This new dynasty expanded its territory in all directions due to the weakness of the later Seleucid kings. Hasmonean John Hyrcanus (134–104 BCE) conquered the territory of Edom (Idumea), the old fraternal enemy of the Jews, and forcibly converted its inhabitants. These military successes brought concomitant economic advantages; the peace that reigned in the country stimulated trade and commercial activity. However, the advancement of the royal family, necessary alliances with the Seleucids, and the increasing power of Rome paradoxically prompted further Hellenistic assimilation, as evidenced by the Hasmoneans' adoption of Greek names.

In the dual position of king and high priest, the Hasmoneans attracted to their coterie the upper reaches of the priestly clan. This nobility comprised a party that would become the Sadducees. Even though the kings were also high priests and many nobles were priests as well, their outlook was worldlier. The Temple service alone was sufficient for them to ensure God would favor the nation, if not the individual Jew.

In the post-Hasmonean world, even after the Roman conquest of Israel (63 BCE) and the establishment of the Herodian monarchy (40 BCE), mystical speculation was limited to fringe elements. Certainly the Hasmonean kings and Herod after them did not encourage messianism. Economic prosperity breeds more focus on enjoying the fruits of this world than contemplation of what is beyond. According to the Mishnah and Josephus (a historian of this period), the upper-class Sadducees denied any existence after death and generally limited religious influence on daily life to the bare minimum of what was prescribed by the Bible. The Pharisees represented a middle-class movement and emphasized intellectual acumen in biblical interpretation with strict adherence to an oral law they developed as a supplement to the Torah. The early Christians considered the Pharisees their main opponents in the struggle to win the minds, hearts, and souls of the Jewish people.[2]

These groups were not the only Jewish denominations at this time. Philo of Alexandria describes a sect of Egyptian Jews, the Therapeutae, dedicated to a life of asceticism and contemplation. Their devotions consisted of fasting, solitary prayer, and Scripture study:

> The entire interval from dawn to evening is given up by them to spiritual exercises. For they read the holy scriptures and draw out in thought and allegory their ancestral philosophy, since they regard the literal meanings as symbols of an inner and hidden nature revealing itself in covert ideas.[3]

In Israel lived a mystical faction similar to the Therapeutae known as the Essenes. Josephus writes of their extreme piety and saintliness, depicting a collective life with the practice of celibacy. Since the discovery of the Dead Sea Scrolls, many scholars have attributed them to this group. It most likely was during the reign of John Hyrcanus that those who might have been Essenes took to Qumran to write their scrolls in the desert away from the desecration of the Temple.[4]

No matter to whom the authorship of the Scrolls is attributed, one can gain insight into the spiritual world of their creators. Life was bound by strict adherence to their code of laws and the communal chanting of hymns and psalms, the nonobservance of which resulted in expulsion. In the Scrolls we're introduced to a universe in terrestrial and cosmic conflict between the forces of light and darkness. This eschatology envisions a final battle, such as those described in Ezekiel and Daniel, in which the angels of good and evil battle alongside human forces with the ultimate victory belonging to the pious members of their sect over non-Jews and impious Jews alike. Interestingly enough, as we will note later, belonging to the side of the angels was marked by certain physiognomy and other external characteristics such as a shapely head.[5]

In the later Merkavah ("Chariot") mysticism texts, we have a work ascribed to Rabbi Yishmael that deals with chiromancy as well as physiognomy. This superficial concern is justified by appealing to Genesis 5:1–2: "In the day that God created man, in the likeness of God made He him . . . and blessed them." Physical appearance is elevated to a Divine attribute. Perhaps the exclusion of those with what were held to be imperfections was influenced also by the biblical prohibition against deformed priests offering sacrifice.[6]

In this period we again encounter a characteristic of the Bnei HaNeviim. People felt the spirit of the Lord and spoke in tongues, a phenomenon mentioned a number of times in the Christian Bible.[7] Acts describes speaking in tongues as a mystical experience that comes upon the individual under the influence of the Holy Spirit. I once met a group of evangelical Christians who spoke in tongues at church. One person initiated the conversation and was joined by others who believed the Holy Spirit had descended.

In the magical texts of this time, we find nonsense syllables and inauthentic foreign words, which seem to be the style in Greek as well as Jewish incantations. Scholem notes that the later Hekhalot texts of Merkavah mysticism, those sometimes quoted as "the Work of the Chariot," exhibit "the sheer gibberish of magical abracadabra."[8] But what may seem nonsense to some can to others be a method of attaining spirituality. One only has to think of the Hare Krishna movement and the repeated chant that fills the devotee with rapture. Similarly this Merkavah would carry a rapturous devotee through the Hekhalot (palaces) to the Divine throne.

After Herod's death, Judea became a province without a king and thus under the direct control of Rome. So hope for a messiah to rescue the people from the yoke of foreign domination became an active force. But the end of days did not come from the Heavens and others seized upon the earthlier alternative of rebellion against Rome, which succeeded only in the 70 CE destruction of the Temple. The revolt was doomed to failure not just because of the enormous might of the Roman Empire but also the civil war between various internal factions, which destroyed each other while Roman legions were at the gate.[9]

The subsequent rabbinic reconstruction of Jewish life instituted by Rabban Yohanan ben Zakkai was facilitated by then-emperor Vespasian's need to have a Jewish partner in rebuilding the community after the devastation of war.[10] The Sanhedrin, which had functioned as the high court of the Jewish people and at whose head sat the Nasi ("Prince"), had been eliminated in the rebellion against Rome. Yohanan established his school in Yavneh and reconstituted the Sanhedrin there. Several of his decrees replaced the centrality of the Temple for both the New Year and Booths festivals.[11] With Rabban Yohanan ben Zakkai, we enter a notable age of Jewish religious development. The rabbis of this time are called Tannaim and this period is called the Tannaitic Age, which encompassed a second failed insurgency against Rome as well as the crowning achievement of the codification of the Oral Law in the composition known as the Mishnah.[12] This systematic compendium of Jewish legal opinions arranged in encyclopedic order seems to have been influenced by Greek logic.

The Hillel branch of the Pharisees, which was inclined to brotherly love and against the war with Rome, was now entrusted by its Roman masters with the pacification of the Jewish community. The elevation of Rabban Gamliel, a great-great-grandson of Hillel the Elder, continued the reign of one family that would lead the people for about four hundred years. Rabban Gamliel ascended to the position of Nasi, but his stern, authoritative manner engendered a rabbinic revolt that temporarily removed him from office.[13] His position as the political and religious leader of the Jews was recognized by his formal investiture from the representative of the Roman Emperor in Syria.[14] Rabban Gamliel is known for ordering the standard prayer called the Eighteen Blessings and the insertion of a special blessing designed to exclude heretics from the congregation.[15]

The House of Hillel (his descendants now rulers of the people), whose founder was a proponent of peace, had an extra incentive to preserve the status quo. The Nasi was in a position of wealth and prestige that did not encourage conflict with the power of Rome. Rabban Gamliel's interest in restructuring Jewish life extended to the substitution of prayer in place of Temple sacrifice as well as limiting thoughts, beliefs, and speculations beyond the pale of normative doctrine.

Rabban Gamliel also promoted the study of Greek, which was the language of the eastern Roman Empire. Obligatory interaction with Roman officials made knowledge of their language and culture beneficial to Jewish leaders. On trips to Rome, Rabban Gamliel and others had occasion to enter into dialogue with philosophers on the nature of God and the problem of evil in the world.[16]

Although Judaism has been attacked by Christian propagandists as esoteric blasphemy or defended by its rational adherents as a religion of law, neither side of this polemic has the whole truth. Two of the foremost legal sages—Rabbis Akiva ben Yosef and Yishmael ben Elisha—engaged in mystical exercises. The loss of the sacrificial cult deprived the people of the vicarious lustration of blood on the altar. The search for a substitute to sacrifice that would provide the same emotional intensity and spiritual ecstasy inspired attempts to recapture the visions of the prophets.

Akiva and Yishmael were responsible for two diametric legal schools. Rabbi Yishmael interpreted the Torah as a document in the ordinary language of human speech. On the other hand Rabbi Akiva regarded each particle of Scripture as having profound meaning, drawing conclusions from the text that, according to the tale of a later Rav, would have astounded Moses.[17] At the same time both Akiva and Yishmael claimed they took journeys to the Heavens that rival in their descriptions Greek and Roman trips to Hell. This condominium of legal expertise and mystical flight is not foreign to the many rabbis we will meet along the way who also combined these seemingly opposite traits.[18]

We must quote extensively from the first chapter of Ezekiel to help illustrate such journeys. The priest and prophet Ezekiel is by the river Chebar in Babylonia when he has a vision of a wind from the north and a great cloud with flashes of lightning:

> [5]And out of the midst thereof came the likeness of four living creatures. And this was their appearance: they had the likeness of a man. [6]And every one had four faces, and every one of them had four wings. [7]And their feet were straight feet; and the sole of their feet was like the sole of a calf's foot; and they sparkled like the colour of burnished brass. [8]And they had the hands of a man under their wings on their four sides; and as for the faces and wings of them four. . . . [10]As for the likeness of their faces, they had the face of a man; and they four had the face of a lion on the right side; and they four had the face of an ox on the left side; they four had also the face of an eagle. [11]Thus were their faces; and their wings were stretched upward; two wings of every one were joined one to another, and two covered their bodies. . . . [13]As for the likeness of the living creatures, their appearance was like coals of fire, burning like the appearance of torches; it flashed up and down among the living creatures; and there was brightness to the fire, and out of the fire went forth lightning. [14]And the living creatures ran and returned as the appearance of a flash of lightning.

Compare the below continuation of Ezekiel with the biblical description of Moses and the elders ascending Mount Sinai: "Then went up Moses, and Aaron, Nadab, and Abihu, and seventy of the elders of Israel; and they saw the God of Israel; and there was under His feet the like of a paved work of sapphire stone, and the like of the very heaven for clearness."[19]

> [24]And when they went, I heard the noise of their wings like the noise of great waters, like the voice of the Almighty, a noise of tumult like the noise of a host; when they stood, they let down their wings. [25]For, when there was a voice above the firmament that was over their heads, as they stood, they let down their wings. [26]And above the firmament that was over their heads was the likeness of a throne, as the appearance of a *sapphire stone*[emphasis added]; and upon the likeness of the throne was a likeness as the appearance of a man upon it above. [27]And I saw as the colour of electrum, as the appearance of fire round about enclosing it, from the appearance of his loins and upward; and from the appearance of his loins and downward I saw as it were the appearance of fire, and there was brightness round about him. [28]As the appearance of the bow that is in the cloud in the day of rain, so was the appearance of the brightness round about. This was the appearance of the likeness of the glory of the Lord. And when I saw it, I fell upon my face, and I heard a voice of one that spoke.

Regarding the plain sense of the passage, Bible scholars in most part agree this is a premonition of the glory of God departing the first Temple as it is being destroyed.[20] As far as mystics were concerned, however, Ezekiel is witness to God's throne. To soften the anthropomorphism of the passage, the appearance of the likeness of a man on the throne is referred to as "the glory of God." This important expression will be met many times as we continue our examination of Jewish mysticism. Mystics who wished to have this vision were referred to as "those who descend to the chariot," later changed to "those who ascend." Coupled with this desire to see God's throne perched on the chariot was a belief that one had to traverse six palaces of Heaven before admission into the seventh where the throne sat.

The idea of seven levels of Heaven and Hell is as old as the Sumerians, one of the first civilizations, and has persisted to our own day thanks to the work of Dante.[21] *Hekhalot Zutarti* (The Lesser Palaces) and *Hekhalot Rabbati* (The Greater Palaces) recount the mystical ascents of Akiva and Yishmael. Some date these texts to the fourth or fifth century CE, years after the demise of these rabbis,[22] but several reasons suggest an earlier date, solidifying the theory that they recorded their own experiences:

- The mystics who treasured these texts allowed into their group only men who met their physiognomic standards, which we first encountered in the Dead Sea Scrolls of the first century BCE.[23]
- The texts have nonsense syllables and made-up, foreign-sounding names and formulae, which are associated with speaking in tongues, found in the Christian Bible as well as in Greek and Aramaic magic incantations. These predate or are contemporaneous with Rabbis Akiva and Yishmael.[24]
- Rabbi Yishmael testifies to his spiritual ascent to Heaven in what must be a vision, for he imagines himself as high priest several decades after the destruction of the Temple when that office ceased to exist.[25]
- In the Talmud passage in which Akiva ascends with his companions, the description of the walls of Heaven is similar to that found in the fourteenth chapter of Enoch.[26]

In tractate Hagigah, Akiva leads a group of four to Paradise. Only Akiva is reported to have returned from the trip intact; the three others suffer death, madness, and apostasy. It may be argued that this tale belongs to legends of Akiva's greatness. However, the negative reflection on the other rabbis and inclusion in both Talmuds lend it credence, as libel against those from Akiva's circle published in two independent texts over three centuries probably would not have been accepted without protest. Does this resemble *folie imposée*, or shared delusion? Rabbi Akiva's dominant position and personality make the possibility intriguing![27]

In this same passage Akiva warns his companions not to say "water." On reaching Heaven, Greek Orphics are to slake their thirst at a special lake. Akiva's warning could be reactive to the Orphic prescription. Note this quotation from Psalms 101:7: "He that speak falsely will not stand before my eyes." Is the meaning that Greeks who think they have reached Heaven are deluded? Akiva seems to have been intimately familiar with the Greek world.[28] His order of the Mishnah bespeaks familiarity with Aristotelian logical classification.[29]

The ascensions of Rabbis Akiva and Yishmael exhibit further Greek influ–ence. The gates to these palaces of Heaven are guarded by fiery angels (Seraphim), but help is afforded the worthy traveler by two main angels. The chief angel is Metatron or Lad, who used to be Enoch but was brought on high to escape the Flood and transformed into gatekeeper of God's throne. The name Metatron has escaped a clear definition or derivation and just might be made up to sound like Greek.

Sefer Hekhalot (Book of the Palaces) depicts trips through the six palaces up to the throne of God. In it Rabbi Yishmael relates his ascent to the seventh Heaven and how Metatron wards off the fiery beings that attempt to bar Yishmael's way. When the rabbi beholds the Merkavah, these destructive angels cast him into a trance, but God silences them and closes their eyes so as not to look upon His beloved Yishmael. In words reminiscent of Daniel's visions, the following is told:

> Rabbi Yishmael said at that time the eagles of the Chariot and the wheels of flame and the Seraphim of consuming fire came and asked Metatron and said to him: "Lad, why was this one born of woman allowed that he should come and gaze on the Chariot. From what people is he? From what tribe is he? What is the nature of this one?" Metatron replied and said to them: "From the people of Israel that The Holy One Blessed Be He chose for himself from the seventy languages. From the tribe of Levi is he who lifts up the heave offering to His Name. From the seed of Aaron is he who The Holy One Blessed Be He chose for himself to be his servant; that The Holy One Blessed Be He by himself tied the crown of priesthood to him on Mount Sinai." Immediately they opened and said: "For sure this one is fit to gaze upon the Chariot, as it is written, 'Happy is the people who are like this. . . .' (Psalms 144:15)."[30]

The intent of these voyagers was to pierce the mystery and obtain the joy of being in the presence of God. In the Talmud one great Amora (teacher of the Talmud and interpreter of the Mishnah) says the only difference between this world and Heaven is that the righteous will sit with crowns on their heads and bask in the radiance of God.[31]

The song of the heavenly bodies in their praise of God, coupled with quotes from Ezekiel's Chariot, are in the first blessing after the call to prayer. On Shabbat, the first blessing before the Shema has the words "He (God) is glorious above the holy beasts; resplendent in glory on the chariot."[32] These mystics left their mark on the liturgy, and anyone reading the morning prayers is introduced to their world.

Hekhalot literature based on earlier Merkavah mysticism usually is dated to the fourth and fifth centuries CE. Many of the hymns of this literature have made their way into the Jewish prayer book. "The majesty and the faithfulness are to He who lives eternally," recited on Yom Kippur and daily in Hasidic circles, is perhaps the best known of this genre.[33]

Rabbi Eliezer ben Yose the Galilean (c. 200 CE) is credited with the development of thirty-two rules for interpreting the Bible, among which are two that reflect Greco-Roman influence. One formula takes numerical values of Hebrew letters, generates sums for words, and relates the word sums to one another. This technique, called gematria, can be used to apply all manner of interpretations to text and is found in the Talmud. The word *gematria* most likely is related to the Greek word for *letter.*

The mystical meaning of numbers is attractive to those who employ Hebrew letters for both words and numbers. One also might speculate that the use of numbers for interpretation could have been influenced by the Pythagorian school of numeric mysticism. About the time of Rabbi Eliezer, legends of Pythagoras were being circulated.[34]

Another interpretive rule of Rabbi Eliezer combines the initial or final letters of words to form new phrases and utilizes the inverse operation as well. This acrostic system, called notarikon, probably was borrowed from the note-taking of Roman scribes. Thus in the Kabbalah the word for "paradise" (*pardes*—orthographically *prds*—in Hebrew) is analyzed as each successive letter designating a deeper form of biblical exegesis: *p* = *pshat* ("simple" meaning); *r* = *remez* ("hint"); *d* = *drash* (homiletic "inquiry"); and *s* = *sod* (mystical "secret"). This may imply that Bible study leads the student closer to paradise. Using notarikon, the Hebrew letters of the first word in the Bible—*Bereishit* ("In the beginning")—spell out "He created firmament, earth, Heavens, sea, abyss." The word *amen* becomes "God is a faithful King." The *Ana BeKoakh* prayer of Nehunya ben HaKanah found in the Friday night liturgy is a word-initial acrostic of verses spelling the forty-two-lettered name of God.[35]

The rabbinic prohibitions classified as the Seven Commandments of the Sons of Noah amount to a jus gentium, or set of laws binding to non-Jews. One of these Noahide Laws, that of not eating flesh torn from a live animal, may not make much sense in a Jewish framework. However, set against the sparagmos, the tearing apart of an animal, and then omophagia, eating it raw, which are part of the cult of Dionysus/Bacchus, the prohibition is contextualized comprehensibly.[36]

Cross-cultural interchange with the Greek world probably was more significant than scholars were willing to admit in the past.

One of the ways in which the Roman world most robustly influenced Jewish life was the legal development that took place in the first two centuries of the Common Era. This was the period of the great commentaries and collections of law brought forth by the Roman jurists Papinian, Ulpian, and Paulus, who were from what is today either Lebanon or Syria. In many ways Jewish and Roman jurists arrived at similar conclusions either by borrowing from each other or independent conclusion. [37] In 212 CE Rome issued the *Lex Caracalla*, making it possible for most inhabitants of the Roman Empire to attain citizenship and thereby appeal their legal difficulties to Roman courts.[38]

All of the above probably were the impetus for Rabbi Yehudah HaNasi (c. 200 CE) to institute a reform of the Jewish legal system and publish the Mishnah; the rabbis did not want Jews to use the Roman courts.[39] The Mishnah and a companion treatise called the Tosefta originated in the school of Rabbi Akiva, and both collections owe their logical formulation of Jewish law to him.[40] It is the Tosefta, however, that particularly reflects his mystical bent.[41]

Rabbi Yehudah HaNasi, the final editor of the Mishnah, made sure to limit any mystical speculation so as to suppress it and he had good reason. Rabbi Akiva, who was recognized as the main proponent of such speculation, also was a supporter of the messianic pretensions of Bar Kokhba (c. 135 CE), who led the Jewish people into an even more devastating rebellion against Rome than the one that preceded it in 70 CE. In retaliation for that revolt, Rome executed many rabbis—who were supposed to keep the peace by subduing Judaism—Rabbi Akiva among them.[42]

Whether or not Rabbi Yehudah was on friendly terms with the Roman Emperor, his wealth and status encouraged him to curb all types of thought, heterodox or not, that would threaten the status quo. As leader of his people, Yehudah protected them from ideas that ultimately could endanger them.[43] So we have in the Mishnah prohibitions against two areas of mystical thought. One deals with the act of creation and the other with Ezekiel and the Work of the Chariot.[44]

I close this chapter with the most controversial book of Merkavah literature: *Shiur Komah* (Measurement of the Height). We have mentioned that to soften the anthropomorphism of the Bible, Jews referred to the Glory of God by which He manifested himself to humans. *Shiur Komah* describes a macroanthropos (giant human), which seems to be the bodily appearance but not the essence of God. This emanation will be identified later when the glory becomes the Shekhinah (God's immanence). This book, which was attacked viciously by the opponents of rabbinic Judaism, sought to deal with the problem of how God, who is spirit, could create the world out of nothing. This will play its part in later mystical speculation.[45]

NOTES

1. 1 Macc. 14:41.

2. For an excellent analysis of Flavius Josephus' and the other sources of this period as well as new insight into Jesus, see John P. Meier, *A Marginal Jew: Rethinking The Historical Jesus,* The Anchor Bible Reference Library (New York: Doubleday, 1991–2009), I–IV.

3. Philo De Vita Contemplativa, par. 28, in "Thereaputae," *Encylopaedia Judaica,* last modified January 2007, http://www.encyclopedia.com/article-1G2-2587519800/therapeutae.html.

4. Mishnah Maaser Sheni 5:15 (see also Jerusalem Talmud thereon). He instituted reforms in the Temple service that this group deemed sacrilegious.

5. See Mladen Popović, *Reading the Human Body: Physiognomics and Astrology in the Dead Sea Scrolls and Hellenistic-Early Roman Period Judaism* (Leiden: Koninklijke Brill NV, 2007), 7. The possibility of chiromancy originating in this period is a matter of conjecture by some scholars.

6. Lev. 21:17–24.

7. Acts 2, 10:46, 19:6 and 1 Cor. 12–14. Perhaps Saul's prophesying in 1 Sam. 10 is an incident of speaking in tongues. The words of the Sybil at Delphi were unintelligible and had to be interpreted by the priests.

8. See Gershom Scholem, *Jewish Gnosticism, Merkabah Mysticism, and the Talmudic Tradition* (New York: The Jewish Theological Seminary of America, 1960) 75 f. and 94–100.

9. See Flavius Josephus, *The Jewish War,* ed. Gaalya Cornfeld (Grand Rapids: Zondervan Publishing House, 1982) II, 180 and xviii, 190 ff.

10. The rabbinic accounts of the meeting between Yohanan and Vespasian are of course legendary. See Gittin 56a–b; Lamentations Rabbah 1:5; Avot D'Rabbi Natan I 422–424; Avot D'Rabbi Natan II 19.

11. Mishnah Rosh HaShanah 4:1; Mishnah Sukkah 3:11.

12. For this period see Gedalyahu Alon, *The Jews in Their Land* (Cambridge: Harvard University Press, 1980).

13. Brakhot 27b–28a.

14. Mishnah Eduyot 7:7.

15. Brakhot 28b.

16. Tosefta Sotah 15:8(4); Sotah 49b; Avodah Zarah 54a–b.

17. Shevuot 26a. For Amora Rav's story see Menahot 29b.

18. See R. J. Zwi Werblowsky, *Joseph Karo: Lawyer and Mystic* (Philadelphia: The Jewish Publication Society of America, 1977). Karo wrote commentaries to Maimonides' Code as well as his chief work, a commentary to the Arba'ah Turim of Jacob ben Asher. Karo's *Shulkhan Arukh,* along with the notes of Moses Isserles, became the standard code for decisors of Jewish Law (Halakhah) even to this day.

19. Exod. 24:10–11.

20. For a study of Ezekiel, see Bernhard W. Anderson, *Understanding the Old Testament* (Upper Saddle River: Prentice Hall), 384–389.

21. See Samuel Noah Kramer, *History Begins at Sumer* (Philadelphia: University of Pennsylvania Press, 1973).

22. See Gershom Scholem, *Major Trends in Jewish Mysticism* (New York: Schocken Books, 1974), ii. However, in *Jewish Gnosticism, Merkabah Mysticism and Talmudic Tradition* (New York: The Jewish Theological Seminary of America, 1960), Scholem concludes that at least the trips to

Heaven, celestial hymns of the Greater Hekhalot, and Shiur Komah could be dated to as early as the Tannaitic period (before 212 CE).

23. See note 2.

24. See ch. 1.

25. Brakhot 7a.

26. See ch. 1.

27. See Hagigah 14b and the psychoanalytic discussion in Danilo Arnone, Anish Patel, and Giles Ming-Yee Tan, "The Nosological Significance of *Folie à Deux:* a Review of the Literature," *Annals of General Psychiatry* 5 (2006):11, doi:10.1186/1744-859X-5-11, ISSN 1744-859X. In his comments to Tractate Hagigah of the Babylonian Talmud. Rashi says that the rabbis ascended by means of the name of God. However, the Tosafot (Franco-German medieval commentators) and David ben Naphtali Fraenkel (1704–1762), in his commentary to the Jerusalem Talmud, Hagigah Chapter 2 Halakhah 1, assert that they did not really ascend to Heaven but only seemed to do so, implying that it was illusional. The fact that it was illusional was first attributed to Hai Gaon by Rabbi Nathan ben Yehiel of Rome in his *Arukh.* See *Aruch Completum Nathan Filio Jechielis,* edited by Dr. Alexander Kohut (Vienna, Austria: Georg Brog, 1878).

28. For the desire to drink water, see W.K.C. Guthrie, *Orpheus and Greek Religion* (Princeton: Princeton University Press, 1993), 177. "Keeping, then to the right, the soul comes to a spring, and addresses to the guardians that are before it a prayer that it may be allowed to drink of the water, of which it is in dire need: 'I am parched with thirst and I perish.'"

29. Sanhedrin 86a. Rabbi Yohanan ben Napha attributes the logical Mishnah to Rabbi Meir as well as the traditional exposition of Midrash to Rabbis Yehudah and Simeon, but all are under the influence of Rabbi Akiva. Rabbi Akiva's disputant and colleague, Rabbi Yishmael, did not use anything but the traditional midrashic form of exposition.

30. *Sefer Hekhalot* (Lvov: 1850), ii, www.hebrewbooks.org.

31. Rav Brakhot 17a.

32. *Siddur Yitzchak Yair HaShalem, Nusach Ashkenaz,* ArtScroll Mesorah Series (Brooklyn: Mesorah Publications, Ltd., 1994), pocket-size edition, 211. Kavod ("glory") at times is used as the seen physical manifestation of God ("His glory fills the world.").

33. See Scholem, *Major Trends,* 57–59 for discussion and translation.

34. See "Pythagoras," *Stanford Encyclopedia of Philosophy,* last modified May 28, 2014, plato.stanford.edu/entries/pythagoras/.

35. "Notarikon," *Jewish Encyclopedia,* http://www.jewishencyclopedia.com/articles/11602-notarikon.

36. Tosefta Avodah Zarah 9:4, as evidenced in Euripides, *The Bacchae.*

37. See Boaz Cohen, *Jewish and Roman Law: A Comparative Study in Two Volumes* (New York: The Jewish Theological Seminary of America, 2012), for striking similarities between Jewish and Roman law.

38. Dio Cassius, *Roman History* LXXVIII, ix.

39. See Mishnah Gittin 9:8 ff.

40. Sanhedrin 86a.

41. See Scholem, op. cit., 42 f.

42. For the life of Akiva, see Louis Finkelstein, *Akiba: Scholar, Saint and Martyr* (New York: Atheneum, 1978).

43. Note the gratuitous denigration of Rabbi Akiva from a Rabbi Yohanan ben Torta in Lamentation Rabbah Parsha 2 Piska 4.

44. For the prohibition on speculative study, see Mishnah Hagigah 2:1.

45. For a description of the book, see Scholem, op. cit., 63–67, but see note xvii for his dating this work possibly as early as the Tannaitic period.

3 The Book of Creation

A New Beginning

Jewish mysticism can be described as having two separate goals that may exist, at times, in concert. One pursuit is the contemplation of God and the joy of piercing the veil, as dangerous as that may be. For we are warned in Exodus 33, as Moses attempts to see God's "face" and is rebuffed:

> "Now therefore, I pray You, if I have found grace in Your sight, show me now Your ways, that I may know You, to the end that I may find grace in Your sight; and consider that this nation is Your people." . . . And the LORD said unto Moses: "I will do this thing also that you have spoken, for you have found grace in My sight, and I know you by name." And he said: "Show me, I pray You, Your glory." . . . And He said: "You cannot see My face, for man shall not see Me and live."[1]

Moses does not want just to see the "face" of God; he wants knowledge of God's ways. So the second goal of Jewish mysticism becomes the search for answers from the beginning of creation including the origin of evil. How could a just and loving God allow evil and suffering to enter the world? This paradox is an overarching problem for the committed Jew. In the second paragraph of the Shema prayer, Jews recite a passage from Deuteronomy, in which the observant are promised, individually and societally, a long life upon the land given to them by God.[2] In the words of Abraham: "Will not the judge of the world do justly?"[3] As the years of exile, persecution, degradation, and massacre drag on, however, God seems to betray the people who repeat His promise morning and evening.

Rabbi Yannai, a student of Rabbi Yehudah HaNasi, confessed by rational conclusion, "We cannot explain why the wicked prosper and even more so why the righteous suffer."[4] The spiritually alert could not accept this inequity, and Jewish mysticism was compelled to take on a messianic component. The solution to the problem of evil, if not achieved in the here and now, had to be deferred to an "End of Days," induced by God alone or with the assistance of human agency.

In his Mishnah, Rabbi Yehudah HaNasi limits speculation not only on the Work of the Chariot, but also on a similar exploration of the mystical elements in the

Work of Creation.[5] The book of Genesis owes its Greek name to Philo (c. 50 BCE–25 CE), a Jewish philosopher of Alexandria, Egypt, and to the Septuagint, a third century BCE Greek translation of the Torah, which called Genesis the "Book of Creation of the World." The early Hebrew name for the first book of the Torah, *Bereishit* ("in the beginning"), still is used by Jews today.[6]

Regarding a text other than Genesis, the Talmud mentions a book of creation, which possibly refers to *Sefer Yetsirah* (Book of Creation), a rabbinic explanation of how creation came into being. No rabbis are mentioned by name, so fixing a date for this mystical work is speculative, but the language of *Sefer Yetsirah* is very close to the Hebrew spoken at the time of the Mishnah (c. 200 CE).[7] The Jewish, Christian, and Pagan Gnostics of this period even circulated a treatise known as "The Creation of the World." Scholars also have suggested an earlier date of publication, noting the similarities between *Sefer Yetsirah* and the magical texts of the second century BCE, which instruct practitioners how to imitate the creative work of God, making occult use of letters.

In the time of the Talmud lived a devotee of mystical speculation widely known by just his title, Rav (175–247 CE). His student, Rav Yehudah the Amora, relates a saying in the name of his teacher that Betzalel, the fashioner of the sanctuary in the wilderness, knew the combination of letters by which the world was created.[8] *Sefer Yetsirah* teaches that God created the world using the twenty-two letters of the Hebrew alphabet and ten numbers, producing thirty-two marvelous paths. The authors use an unusual Hebrew term for number, *sefor(a)*, which in the later Kabbalah becomes the ten Sefirot, or emanations by which the world comes into being. To harmonize the Jewish doctrine of creation from nothing with the pagan idea of primordial elements, *Sefer Yetsirah* has the Spirit of God produce three potentialities that are realized as fundamental elements. Space, representing six dimensions of three paired opposites, also manifested before creation. The one Spirit of God, three elements, and six spatial dimensions become the ten Sefirot, which exist only in abstraction. The Spirit of God is the end as well as the beginning of the Sefirot. At no point is the Spirit of God absent from the process.

According to Bereishit, creation comes into being through God's utterances, which are a precise combination of Hebrew letters. Likewise, in *Sefer Yetsirah*, the twenty-two letters of the Hebrew alphabet produce the material world, and the ten Sefirot usher creation from potentiality to actuality. The ten Sefirot and the twenty-two letters are thus described in the first sentence of the book: "the thirty-two paths . . . God had engraved. . . ." God is likened to a sculptor who chisels beauty out of a formless mass. The Sefirot, which are formless essences, are anchored by the forms of letters to the real world, which is both essence and form.[9] Suffice it to say the ten Sefirot become the main thrust of Kabbalistic speculation.

The mysticism of the chariot and creation was native to the Jewish centers of

Israel and Babylonia. The Israeli center was diminished over the centuries following the conversion of Constantine to Christianity and the successive Christian emperors' persecution of Judaism, as finalized in the Code of Justinian.[10] Rav brought the traditions of mystical exploration from Israel to Babylonia, which were continued by his spiritual descendants, and the lands of the Babylonian exile became epicenters of Jewish scholarship. The great Yeshivot (academies) of Sura and Pumbeditha, which produced the Babylonian Talmud, flourished until the second millennium (the transfer from Zoroastrian to Islamic hegemony had no significant effect on the situation of the Jews). Among the best-known *Sefer Yetsirah* commentators is Saadia Gaon (882–942 CE), the most famous head of the Academies of Babylonia after the redaction of the Talmud. Two other commentators, Rabbis Abraham ben David and Moses ben Nahman (known as Nahmanides and by his acronym, Ramban), were primarily responsible for the development of the later Kabbalah.[11]

However, what was in the east did not stay in the east. In 797 CE, Charlemagne, who would be crowned Holy Roman Emperor three years later, sent a Jew named Isaac on a mission to the Abbasid Khalif Haroun Al Rashid, the great Iraqi ruler celebrated for his cultural developments.[12] Jewish life moved westward from the centers that saw the formation of its chief literature and creed to the lands of the former Roman Empire and the Germanic territory that resisted the legions of Rome. The western dawn of Jewish learning would pave new avenues in rabbinic mysticism.

An outstanding example of the medieval Franco-German (Ashkenaz) school, Rabbi Shelomoh ben Yitshak (1040–1105 CE), known by his acronym, Rashi, is the preeminent Jewish commentator on the Bible and Babylonian Talmud. In Rashi's commentary to the talmudic tractate Sanhedrin (page 65b), he tells a story of Babylonian brothers Rav Hoshaiah and Rav Hanina (c. 350 CE). These Amoraim, rabbis who explicated the Mishnah, were said to create and eat a calf of three years every Sabbath eve. Rashi writes that using the formulae of a book, the two rabbis shared this experience of creation.[13] Scholarly opinion cannot pronounce with certainty that he is referring to *Sefer Yetsirah*. Interestingly, on this folio page of the Babylonian Talmud, another famous sage of the same era, Rava, states that if the righteous wished, they could create the world. To prove his point he created a man whom he sent to Rabbi Zeira. On speaking to the man, Zeira found him mute, saying, "You are from our colleagues; return to your dust," and the creature returned to dust. On the same page Rabbi Akiva states that purposeful fasting can raise a person to a state of purity, implying that fasting was one of the means of triggering a mystical state. At this point the Talmud is discussing the differences between magic and mysticism. Magic transforms or affects other individuals and objects. Mysticism transports its practitioners to a different sphere of reality.

NOTES

1. Exod. 33:13, 17, 18, 20.

2. Deut. 11:13–21.

3. Gen. 18:25.

4. Mishnah Avot 4:19.

5. Mishnah Hagigah 2:1.

6. "Genesis, the Book of," *Jewish Encyclopedia,* http://www.jewishencyclopedia.com/articles/6580-genesis-the-book-of.

7. Talmud Bavli Sanhedrin 65a. See Scholem, *Major Trends*, 75–78.

8. Talmud Bavli Brakhot 55a.

9. "Yezirah, Sefer ('Book of Creation')," *Jewish Encyclopedia,* http://www.jewishencyclopedia.com/articles/13386-sefer-yezirah.

10. "Justinian," *Jewish Encyclopedia,* http://www.jewishencyclopedia.com/articles/9097-justinian.

11. See "Abraham ben David of Posquières (RABaD III.)," *Jewish Encyclopedia,* http://www.jewishencyclopedia.com/articles/420-abraham-ben-david-of-posquieres, and "Moses ben Nahman Gerondi (RaMBaN; known also as Nahmanides and Bonastruc da Porta)," *Jewish Encyclopedia,* http://www.jewishencyclopedia.com/articles/11129-moses-ben-nahman-gerondi.

12. "Charlemagne," *Jewish Encyclopedia,* http://www.jewishencyclopedia.com/articles/4250-charlemagne. See also Salo Wittmayer Baron, *A Social and Religious History of the Jews* (New York: Columbia University Press, 1958), 2nd ed., VI, 45.

13. See Sanhedrin 65b. A shared delusion is called a *folie à deux* in scientific terms. A psychologist friend assured me that the two rabbis who believed they created, cooked, and ate a calf on Sabbath eve could even share the indigestion! Dr. Robert M. Gordon, Ph.D., ABPP Board Certified in Clinical Psychology and Psychoanalysis in Psychology, telephone conversation with author, August 13, 2014. See also ch. 2 note 24.

4 Brilliance and Piety
Along the Banks of the Rhine

Merkavah mysticism left its mark on Jewish worship, especially the High Holy Day services, by popularizing poetry in prayer. In Christian Israel and later Western Europe among the Ashkenazim (Franco-German Jews), this liturgical genre functioned pedagogically to preserve Jewish scholarship and spirituality. Israeli Jews were subject to increasing pressure from the Christian Emperors of the Eastern Roman Empire. The decrees and Code of Justinian, who ruled from 527–565 CE, prohibited the Jewish interpretation of scripture in the synagogue.[1] This interference in the teaching of normative rabbinic tradition compelled poetic liturgists to conceal hints of law and lore in their stanzas.

The Jews did not need to seek asylum from Justinian's legacy. Due to their rabbinically regulated business practices and reliable connections, Jews were invited to commercialize Charlemagne's southwestern German and northern French territories and develop the Rhine as a trade waterway. They settled in riverside towns such as Speyer, Worms, and Mainz, which was one of Charlemagne's two capitals.[2] In Mainz Rabbeinu Gershom bar Yehudah established his academy (c. 900), which produced the most prolific medieval scholars, including Rashi, his grandchildren, and their disciples, whose commentaries inhabit every folio page of the Babylonian Talmud.[3]

For Ashkenazim life was governed by learning and adherence to the rulings of ancient rabbis. Juxtaposing this legal expertise was a flourishing a spiritual world of intense piety, forged in the crucible of the Crusades. Ostensibly initiated to free the Holy Land from Moslem rule, the campaigns turned into a bloodbath for the Jews of Franco-Germany and England. Many Jews took their own lives rather than submit to baptism or murder.[4] The Crusaders' fanaticism was met in kind by the zeal of those who slaughtered their children and wives before turning the knife upon themselves. Their martyrdom left an indelible impression upon the Jews of Ashkenaz.

Out of this maelstrom arose a movement known as Hasidei Ashkenaz (the Pious Men of Germany), founded by Rabbi Yehudah ben Samuel of Regensburg (1150–1217) and his disciple, Rabbi Eleazar ben Yehudah (1165–1230). Rabbi

Eleazar, who lost his wife and children in one of the massacres, was a poetic liturgist and author of legal and mystical books.[5] He wrote a commentary to *Sefer Yetsirah,* which includes astrological analysis and precise instruction on the creation of an artificial human being.[6] In one of his first comments, he employs gematria to prove that God created one-hundred ninety-six worlds, quoting a Merkavah text with the Hebrew word for "worlds," the sum of whose letters is one-hundred ninety-six.[7] He probably was referencing Rabbi Abbahu, who says in a midrash that God created and destroyed worlds before he created Earth. The force of these comments vitiates a literal interpretation of the first chapters of Genesis and allows for the speculation of later mystics.[8]

Considering the persecution and pillage they endured, many Jews felt distrust and contempt for their Christian neighbors. A Jewish practice developed of insulting unknowing Gentiles in Hebrew, which Rabbi Yehudah condemned. In his *Book of the Pious,* he asserts it is a sin to cheat, defraud, or insult a non-Jew, even and especially if the Gentile does not know what is being said.[9]

The Hasidei Ashkenaz emphasized pietistic living, scrupulous commitment to the performance of commandments, and voluntary mortification of the flesh, a Jewish novelty borrowed from Christian practice.[10, 11] Rabbi Yehudah said that as was the custom of the Gentiles, so did the Jews.[12] The *Book of the Pious* is filled with tales of magic and wonder that run parallel to Christian mythology, drawing on common folklore.[13] One interesting fable tells of those who went to the cemetery at the close of the autumnal Sukkot holiday and heard the souls coming forth from their graves to pray for the Jewish community.[14] According to the testimony of Widukind, Abbot of Corvey (c. 980), there existed among German Christians the exact opposite custom, a time-honored ceremony of the living praying to the dead on the first of October.[15]

Advising on the achievement of piety, Rabbi Yehudah urged his audience to be warriors against temptation in the vigor of youth, so as they grew in years, the pattern would be set:

> Piety is hard for a man to achieve. It is better to begin in one's youth, as it is said: "Remember your Creator in the days of your youth," (Ecclesiastes 12:1). Even when he grows old, he will not depart from it. For the repentance of an old man, when he is old and his desires diminish, is like a man who speaks slander and his tongue fails him, and he does not speak again.[16]
>
> The repentance of a man in his strength and his vigor when his impulse to do evil overpowers him and he conquers it, that is the most praiseworthy repentance . . . and for anything that is difficult for a man and he does it, his reward is very great.[17] Ben Zoma said: ". . . who is a hero? He who conquers his desires. . . ."[18]

The drives of sex and aggression are strongest in our youth, but piety is not just about overcoming them and growing older. The rabbis were aware of the importance of channeling these impulses in order to build and populate the world.[19]

Rabbis Yehudah and Eleazar also contributed to the liturgy of the Ashkenazic synagogue. The "Song of the Glory," "Hymns of Unity," and other works attributed to them accentuate the glory by which humans experience God. In the "Song of the Glory," God is described as both a strong, handsome young man of war and a wise old sage in judgment. Yehudah rectifies the contradiction between varied anthropomorphic Divine imagery and God's supreme constancy with the words "You are One in all depictions."[20]

Another interesting work that scholars date around the time of Hasidei Ashkenaz is *Sefer HaBahir* (Book of Brilliance), which names the first three Sefirot.[21] *Keter Elyon* (High Crown) emits *Hokhmah* (Wisdom), which emits *Binah* (Understanding), from which the seven subsidiary Sefirot draw down the Divine into the world.[22]

Sefer HaBahir introduces the doctrine of soul transmigration, answering the age-old question of theodicy: Why do bad things happen to good people? Rabbi Rehumai, an apparent invention of the author, responds that the righteous man was evil in the past and is punished now. His students protest: How can someone be punished for the sins of his youth? The Rabbi responds with the parable of a person planting a vineyard that yields inferior grapes. The planter uproots and replants vine after vine in the same plot until he produces superior wine. So God causes the souls to go from body to body until complete righteousness is achieved.[23]

The scholarship and piety of Ashkenaz became the standard for Jews of northern Europe even after they were expelled or driven from the lands of the west to the east. Our study of mysticism now takes us to southern France and the Iberian Peninsula.

NOTES

1. "Justinian," Jewish Encylopedia, http://www.jewishencyclopedia.com/articles/9097-justinian.
2. "Germany," *Jewish Encyclopedia*, http://www.jewishencyclopedia.com/articles/6603-germany.
3. "Rashi (Soloman bar Issac)," *Jewish Encyclopedia*, http://www.jewishencyclopedia.com/articles/12585-rashi-solomon-bar-isaac and "Tosafot ('additions')," *Jewish Encyclopedia*, http://www.jewishencyclopedia.com/articles/14457-tosafot.
4. See A.M. Habermann, ed., *The Book of Memoirs, Penitential Prayers and Lamentations of Ephraim bar Jacob of Bonn* (Jerusalem: Bialik Institute, 1970). Jewish suicide during the Crusades is compared to the biblical sacrifice of Isaac.
5. "Eleazar ben Judah Kalonymus of Worms," *Jewish Encyclopedia*, http://www.jewishencyclopedia.com/articles/5542-eleazar-ben-judah-ben-kalonymus-of-worms.

6. Commentary on *Sefer Yetsirah* (Przemyśl: Zupnik and Knoller, 1888), 15b, HebrewBooks.org, http://hebrewbooks.org/pdfpager.aspx?req=37671&st=&pgnum=34.

7. Ibid., 1b, HebrewBooks.org, http://hebrewbooks.org/pdfpager.aspx?sits=1&req=37671&st=%u05E2%u05D5%u05DC%u05DE%u05D9%u05DD.

8. Midrash Gen. Rabbah Parsha 9, http://www.daat.ac.il/daat/tanach/raba1/9.htm on Gen. 1:31. "'God saw all that He had done and behold it was very good.' Rabbi Abahu said: From this (we learn) the Holy One Blessed Be He was creating worlds and destroying them, creating them and destroying them, until He created these. He said: 'These pleased Me. Those did not please Me.'" See Scholem, *Major Trends,* 32 and the first comments of Rashi to Gen. 1.

9. Reuven Margoliot, ed., *Sefer Hasidim*, HebrewBooks.org, http://www.hebrewbooks.org/pdfpager.aspx?req=41862&hilite=6edc230b-1cc3-4259-9c9c-fe31f.21bc5de&st=%D7%92%D7%95%D7%99&pgnum=321.

10. "Flagellants," Catholic Encylopedia, http://www.catholic.org/encyclopedia/view.php?id = 4713. "And, undoubtedly, the practice of self-flagellation, familiar to the folk as the ascetic custom of the more severe orders (such as the Camaldolese, the Cluniacs, the Dominicans), had but to be connected in idea with the equally familiar penitential processions popularized by the Mendicants about 1233, to prepare the way for the great outburst of the latter half of the thirteenth century."

11. Reuven Margoliot, ed., Sefer Hasidim, HebrewBooks.org, http://www.hebrewbooks.org/pdfpager.aspx?req=41862&hilite=6edc230b-1cc3-4259-9c9c-fe31f.21bc5de&st=%D7%92%D7%95%D7%99&pgnum=43, and http://www.hebrewbooks.org/pdfpager.aspx?req=41862&hilite=6edc230b-1cc3-4259-9c9c-fe31f.21bc5de&st=%D7%92%D7%95%D7%99&pgnum=284.

12. Reuven Margoliot, ed., *Sefer Hasidim*, HebrewBooks.org, http://hebrewbooks.org/pdfpager.aspx?req=41862&hilite=6edc230b-1cc3-4259-9c9c-fe31f.21bc5de&st=%D7%92%D7%95%D7%99&pgnum=470.

13. See Joseph Dan, *Rabbi Judah the Pious and Caesarius of Heisterbach: Common Motifs in Their Stories*, Scripta Hierosolymitana XXII, eds. Joseph Heinemann and Dov Noy (Jerusalem: The Hebrew University Magnes Press, 1971). According to Dan both drew from common sources without directly influencing each other, proving Judah's statement "as the Gentiles, so did the Jews."

14. Reuven Margoliot, ed., *Sefer Hasidim*, HebrewBooks.org, http://www.hebrewbooks.org/pdfpager.aspx?req=41862&hilite=6edc230b-1cc3-4259-9c9c-fe31f.21bc5de&st=%D7%92%D7%95%D7%99&pgnum=253.

15. "All Hallows Eve," *Catholic Encyclopedia,* http://www.catholic.org/encyclopedia/view.php?id=496.

16. Mishnah Sotah I:7.

17. Reuven Margoliot, ed., *Sefer Hasidim*, HebrewBooks.org, http://www.hebrewbooks.org/pdfpager.aspx?req=41862&hilite=05f.a6f.4d-5d6e-4ad2-a242-944f.4311cb0c&st=%D7%AA%D7%A9%D7%95%D7%91%D7%94&pgnum=40. He mentions here again that it is a sin to lead a non-Jew astray by false information.

18. Mishnah Avot IV:1.

19. See Midrash Gen. Rabbah 9:9. Rabbi Nahman bar Samuel quotes his father: Marriage and building are beneficial products of the "evil impulse."

20. "Shir HaKavod" (Song of the Glory) found at the end of the Sabbath morning service in traditional liturgry. *Siddur Yitzchak Yair HaShalem, Nusach Ashkenaz*, ArtScroll Mesorah Series (Brooklyn: Mesorah Publications, Ltd., 1994) pocket-size edition, 220 f.

21. Scholem, *Major Trends,* 74f. Scholem's views on the *Bahir* have been challenged by later scholarship.

22. "Bahir (full title, *Sefer Ha-Bahir* = 'The Luminous Book'), or Midrash R. Nehunya ben Ha-Kanah," *Jewish Encyclopedia,* http://www.jewishencyclopedia.com/articles/2360-bahir.

23. *Sefer Bahir* (Vilna: 1912), HebrewBooks.org, http://hebrewbooks.org/pdfpager.aspx?req=38017&st=&pgnum=38. Reincarnation as a doctrine of the Pharisees is mentioned by Josephus, *The Jewish War,* II, viii, 142.

תפארת

5 Languedoc and Catalonia

The Kabbalah Takes Form

Our scene now turns to the southeastern French province of Languedoc bordering Catalonia in northeastern Spain, where in the twelfth and thirteenth centuries, a culture flourished that included Catholics, heretical Christians (known as Cathars), Jews, and Moslems. The Cathars believed in a dual Divinity: the evil God of the Old Testament, who created the physical world, and Jesus, the good God of the New Testament who ushered the spiritual realm into existence. They also believed in reincarnation, a conviction some scholars trace back to the Greek Orphics and Pythagoreans of the fifth century BCE.[1] Josephus writes that the Pharisees of the first century BCE held this belief as well.[2]

Rabbi Abraham ben David of Posquières (1125–1198 CE), known by his acronym, Rabad, was a great commentator and philanthropist dedicated to education. Seeking to seize his sizeable assets, the Lord of Posquières wrongfully imprisoned the Rabad, but the Viscount of Carcassonne, who was tolerant of the Jewish and Cathar minorities, intervened and liberated him. The diversity of the city of Carcassonne resulted in its depopulation during the Cathar Crusade of 1209.

The Rabad is the attributed author of an exegesis on *Sefer Yetsirah*. In his commentary to the first passage, he contends that all God created in this world is matched with analogous creation in man. The ten fingers of man, five on one hand and five on the other, represent the ten Sefirot with the heart as the seat of intelligence in the middle.[3] He derives this from the verse "Let us make man in our image, like our form."[4] Thus man is able to discern from what is revealed that which is hidden (mystical lore). As in an anatomy textbook whose pages unfold from the skin to the bones, so one can penetrate beyond the Sefirot in an attempt to perceive the generator of creation, God who is the source of all being.

A master of Jewish law, the Rabad did not hesitate to declare mystical assertions counter to the regnant opinion of his contemporaries. For example it is forbidden for Jews to ascend the Temple Mount, because they are in an impure state requiring a purification ritual rendered impossible by the destruction of the Second Temple. He issued a leniency and ruled that the sanctity of the Temple

Mount was abrogated, claiming: "This has been revealed to me by God's mysterious instruction."[5]

The Rabad is best known for his commentaries, including notes to twelfth-century Spanish polymath Maimonides' code, *Mishneh Torah* (Repetition of the Law). Telling is his comment on the passage in which Maimonides, the supreme rationalist, declares anyone who believes God has a physical form to be a heretic.[6] The Rabad notes that many wiser men than Maimonides believed God had a physical form, and how dare Maimonides call such men heretics![7] Of the more startling anthropomorphic descriptions of God, as found among the sages of the Talmud, is the story of Rabbi Yishmael's ascent to heaven, his dialogue with God, and God's request to be blessed by him.[8] In his commentary to *Sefer Yetsirah*, the Rabad rejects the idea of God having a physical form but, being aware of others of great learning who may have held this belief, rose to their defense.

In the year of the emancipated Rabad's death, religiopolitical turbulence stripped freedom from all the Jews of Christian Europe. Languedoc, previously encompassed by the county of Toulouse, was independent from the French monarchy and attracted organized dissidents, presenting a threat to both crown and church. Pope Innocent III, who reigned from 1198 to 1216, sent a papal legate from Rome to end Catharism through diplomacy and proselytism. After excommunicating the Count of Toulouse for his open support of Cathar independence, Innocent's legate was assassinated in 1208, presumably by supporters of the Count. The Pope capitalized on this murder to launch an excessively violent military campaign against the Cathars and nearly exterminated them over the course of two decades.[9] Innocent then directed his fury at the Jewish population, which was thought to abet heretical movements through contact. The Fourth Lateran Council enacted the ghetto and the badge to separate Jews from the Christian population.[10]

Just as Hasidei Ashkenaz rose from the flames of the Crusades, so too the Cathar Crusade produced the father of Kabbalah. The Rabad's son, Isaac the Blind (1160–1235), is credited as the originator of those speculations and formulations that were to be known, in the full sense of the word, as the Kabbalah ("receiving"). This is a technical distinction between earlier Jewish mysticism and that which developed in the wake of Isaac's ideas. He is important for the reintroduction of the belief in reincarnation and for being the first—among what was to become the Kabbalah of Provence, Catalonia, and Spain—to elaborate on the ten Sefirot.[11]

The Sefirot can be visualized as a fountain. Water streams to different levels, but at the bottom pool, the waters return to the top by the same means they dropped down. The closed circuit is in continuous motion, top down and bottom up. Thus the Sefirot flow from God, the Infinite One who fills creation as the waters of the fountain, all returning to Him. Isaac's work was carried on by his student,

Azriel ben Menahem of Gerona (1160–1238), who was the first to call God—as the origin of this process of creation, which is never diminished—the Ain Sof (Infinite One, lit. "without end").

Azriel wrote *Ezrat Adonai*, a commentary on the ten Sefirot in the form of questions and answers, following the speculative method of philosophy. Like Maimonides he believed God could only be known in a negative way: "The Being that is the originator of all things can have no intention, desire, thought, word, or action. He is infinite; the negation of all negations; the Endless."[12]

Azriel envisaged the world in terms of its latency. He uses the metaphor of sparks proceeding from a lump of coal, but there is no end and no beginning, like a candle that burns forever and lights other wicks, which do not detract from the source flame. Creation was not something new, but rather the transformation of the potential to the actual. The emanations gradually brought forth, through their gradations, physical actuality from the first three Sefirot, "the world of thought;" through the next three Sefirot, "the world of the soul;" to the last four Sefirot, "the material world." Most of the names for the last seven Sefirot are accredited to him.[13]

Azriel was the teacher of Rabbi Moses ben Nahman (1194–1270), known by his acronym, Ramban. The Ramban lived in Gerona, Catalonia, and died in Israel. He was the foremost talmudic authority of his time. Now he chiefly is known for his last work, a lengthy commentary on the Torah. His voluminous writings include commentaries on the Babylonian Talmud in the style of Rashi as well as legal treatises. His prestige dignified the study of Kabbalah with an aura that still attracts talmudic students.

As with so many Jewish masters of the law, the Ramban was a mystic who expressed his thoughts not only in learned treatises but also in poetry:

> From the beginning of time, through eternities I was among
> his hidden treasures.
> From Nothing he called me forth, but at the end of time
> I shall be reclaimed by the King.

(This motif echoes in the morning preliminary prayer: "O My God, the soul that you have set in me is pure, you have created it. . . . You will reclaim it from me and restore it to me in the life to come." This belief in the pre-existence of souls is found as early as the Apocrypha.)[14]

> My life flows from the depth of the spheres
> Which give order and form to the soul;
> Divine forces build it and nourish it;
> Then it is preserved in the chambers of the King.

(The soul may be regarded as a female companion to the King, either a member of the harem or perhaps a princess, as in the expression "all the glory of the King's daughter is within [the palace].")[15]

> He radiated light to bring her forth,
> In hidden wellsprings, right and left.
> The soul descended the ladder of heaven,
> From the primeval pool of Siloam to the garden of the King.[16]

(The soul happily travels through the Sefirot and undergoes travail, knowing its ultimate destination is unification with the Master.)[17]

The Spanish school of Kabbalah soon became the most influential, and its crowning achievement was the publication of the *Zohar*, the most important work in all kabbalistic literature.[18]

NOTES

1. W.K.C. Guthrie, *Orpheus and Greek Religion* (Princeton: Princeton University Press, 1993), 164–172, on Plato *Phaedo*, 70c.

2. See War III notes, Flavius Josephus *The Jewish War*, ed. Gaalya Cornfeld (Grand Rapids: Zondervan Publishing House, 1982), 154: "Their souls remaining spotless and obedient, are allotted the most holy place in heaven, whence in the revolution of ages, they return to find in chaste bodies a new habitation."

3. Rabad, commentary, *Sefer Yetsirah* (Jerusalem: Lewin-Epstein, 1965), ch. 1 mishnah 1, HebrewBooks.org, http://www.hebrewbooks.org/pdfpager.aspx?req=14434&st=&pgnum=28.

4. Gen. 1:26.

5. Salo Wittmayer Baron, *A Social and Religious History of the Jews* (New York: Columbia University Press, 1958), 2nd ed., VIII, 41. See pp. 292 f, note 45, for relevant passages, some of which have been eliminated by copyists.

6. "Moses ben Maimon (RaMBaM; usually called Maimonides)," *Jewish Encyclopedia*, http://www.jewishencyclopedia.com/articles/11124-moses-ben-maimon. In *The Guide for the Perplexed*, Maimonides maintains his own mystical belief in the ability of man to achieve spiritual perfection and prophecy.

7. Rambam *Mishneh Torah*, ed. Naftali Hertz (Lvov: 1810), Sefer Mada Hilkhot Teshuvah, ch. 3 halakhah 7, HebrewBooks.org, http://www.hebrewbooks.org/pdfpager.aspx?req=40449&st=&pgnum=108.

8. Brakhot 7a.

9. "Cathari," Catholic Online, http://www.catholic.org/encyclopedia/view.php?id=2665 and "Albigenses," Catholic Online, http://www.catholic.org/encyclopedia/view.php?id=415.

10. Solomon Grayzel, *The Church and the Jews in the Thirteenth Century* (Philadelphia: Dropsie College for Hebrew and Cognate Learning, 1933) and Robert Chazen, *Church, State and Jew in the Middle Ages* (West Orange: Behrman House, 1980).

11. Scholem, *Major Trends*, 220f and 402 note 55.

12. "Azriel (Ezra) ben Menahem (ben Solomon)," *Jewish Encyclopedia*, http://www.jewishencyclopedia.com/articles/2224-azriel-ezra-ben-menahem-ben-solomon.

13. Ibid.

14. "Preexistence," *Jewish Encyclopedia,* http://www.jewishencyclopedia.com/articles/12339-preexistence, and "Soul (equivalent to the Latin 'anima' and 'spiritus')," *Jewish Encyclopedia,* http://www.jewishencyclopedia.com/articles/13933-soul.

15. Ps. 45:14.

16. Michael Sachs, *Die religioese Poesie der Juden in Spanien,* 2 Aufl. (1901), 50f in Scholem, *Major Trends,* 240.

17. See Rabbi Elazar ben Moshe Azikiri, "Yedid Nefesh," *Siddur Yitzchak Yair HaShalem, Nusach Ashkenaz,* ArtScroll Mesorah Series (Brooklyn: Mesorah Publications, Ltd., 1994) pocket-size edition, 260. The fluid personality of the soul undergoes a metamorphosis from male slave to female lover to son and finally becomes all Israel reunited with God.

18. "Moses ben Nahman Gerondi (RaMBaN; known also as Nahmanides and Bonastruc da Porta)," *Jewish Encyclopedia,* http://www.jewishencyclopedia.com/articles/11129-moses-ben-nahman-gerondi.

חסד

6 Off the Beaten Track

Abraham Abulafia

At the same time the ideas initiated by Isaac the Blind were gaining traction in Spain, a different kabbalistic path opened under the influence of one of the most interesting Jewish mystics of the Middle Ages.

With the knowledge of meditation from yoga and Buddhist sources, many people today become interested in further pursuing spiritual regimens. Little known to them is that one of the earliest practitioners of meditation was Abraham Abulafia, a Spanish Jew. Abulafia, who was born in 1240 in Zaragoza, studied Bible and Talmud with his father. In 1260, after his father's untimely death, Abulafia began a life of travels that took him to the Near East. He also became an avid follower of Maimonides and wrote commentaries on *The Guide for the Perplexed*. In the *Guide* Maimonides speaks of one attaining prophetic status by achieving union with the "Active Intellect of the Universe" that is God. Upon returning to Spain in 1270, Abulafia held on to many of Maimonides' ideas and also took instruction from a cantor, Baruch Togarmi.[1]

Togarmi belonged to a mystical circle that believed they could uncover profound mysteries of the universe and God by means of gematria, notarikon, and temurah (the interchanging of letters to form a new word).[2] Togarmi wrote a commentary to *Sefer Yetsirah*, "The Keys to Kabbalah," which is described by Abulafia in his volume, *The Treasure of the Hidden Eden*.

Abulafia developed a system of mystical meditation that was not dissimilar to the guided meditation practiced by some today. Among Abulafia's almost fifty compositions are *The Life of the World to Come*, *Light of the Higher Intellect*, and *Book of the Desire for the Divine*. His works are prompted by a desire not only to achieve prophecy and mystical experience for himself, but also an equally important desire to share these techniques with those who would follow him. In his works he describes how to prepare and follow his path to achieve an apparition, or a figure that represents one's own image as a light form, and at the same time might be God speaking to the mystic through this vision of the mystic's own form.

Fasting, wearing white garments (as with funeral shrouds and on the Day of Atonement), and donning tefillin (prayer boxes with verses of scripture within), one also may meditate on permutations and combinations of the Hebrew letters, including those that make up the four-letter name of God. We have followed the use of the Hebrew alphabet in mystical thought from the speaking in tongues of the first century through the syllables of the Merkavah mystics, and now down to Abulafia.[3]

Abulafia describes that, before experiencing the sublime peace, the devotee first experiences fear and trembling. According to Abulafia one needs a Master to unlock the soul of the initiate and allow the student to proceed along the spiritual path. The path of Abulafia bears such important similarities to eastern techniques that one has to wonder if, in his travels in the east, he came in contact with those who knew the systems of meditation of India and Tibet.[4] For example the experience of creating the vision of a form in front of oneself is a *tulpa*, a practice known to Tibetan lamas.[5]

Similar to the modern western following of ancient eastern mindfulness practices, the sensual imagery in "The Song of Songs" has pervaded popular culture. Rabbi Akiva interpreted it as the love song between God and Israel. Abulafia, in the footsteps of Togarmi, who spoke of the "Divine Kiss," goes even further in using the image of sexual intercourse as a metaphor for the union of the "Active Intellect" with the soul. According to the rabbis and Maimonides, the "Divine Kiss" preceded the death of the righteous (such as Miriam, Moses, and Aaron) and also might be obtained in life by the adept ecstatic. This idea is developed by Abulafia in his books, *Book of the Key to the Sefirot, Treasure of the Hidden Ede*n, and *Life of the Soul.* [6]

Abulafia came to an interesting end. In 1280, under prophetic inspiration, he decided to meet with Pope Nicholas III in Rome. The Pope was in Suriano and gave orders for a stake to be prepared as a warm reception for Abulafia. Undeterred by this news, Abulafia continued on his journey toward Rome, but before he could reach his destination, Pope Nicholas III died of apoplexy, which, for Abulafia, was a stroke of good luck. These events are detailed by Abulafia himself in *The Book of Testimony.* He writes that it was in his ninth year of prophecy that he resolved to go to the Pope in Rome. In this book, he defends a strict monotheism against the trinitarian beliefs of the Church.[7]

Abulafia then went south to Sicily and was prophesying actively in Messina and Palermo. There, however, he was denounced for considering himself to be a prophet and perhaps Messiah. Rabbi Shelomoh ben Adret, one of the great Jewish legal scholars of the time, did his best to subvert any of Abulafia's teaching. It is only in our age that Abulafia has again come to the attention of so many. The last decade of his life was very fruitful, with prolific writings that have been published recently. It is believed that Abraham Abulafia died somewhere around 1290.[8]

NOTES

1. See Scholem, *Major Trends*, 127.

2. Temurah is done easily in Hebrew, because the twenty-two letters of the alphabet are treated as consonants. The most used system of temurah is "ATBASH," in which the first letter is changed to the twenty-second letter, the second letter is changed to the twenty-first letter, and so on. See Fred Skolnik and Michael Berenbaum, eds., *Encyclopaedia Judaica,* 2nd edition, vol. 7 (New York: Macmillan Reference USA and Jerusalem: Keter Publishing, 2007), "Gematria," 424–447.

3. See Scholem, *Major Trends,* 138–144.

4. Ibid., 139.

5. A Bodhisattva (a being who has attained the high degree of spiritual perfection immediately below that of a Buddha) is the basis of countless magic forms. By the power generated in a state of perfect concentration of mind, he may at one and the same time show a phantom—the *tulpa* (written "*sprulpa*")—of himself in thousands of millions of worlds. He may create not only human forms, but any forms he chooses, even those of inanimate objects. The theory sanctioned in these lines by the highest authority of official Lamaism is identical with that expounded in the Mahayanist literature, where it is said that an accomplished Bodhisattva is capable of effecting ten kinds of magic creations. The power of producing magic formations, *tulkus*, or less lasting and materialized tulpas, does not, however, belong exclusively to such mystic exalted beings. Any human, divine, or demoniac being may be possessed of it. The only difference comes from the degree of power, and this depends on the strength of the concentration and the quality of the mind itself. See Alexandra David-Néel, *Magic and Mystery in Tibet* (London: John Lane Company, 1931), 115.

6. See Moshe Idel, *The Mystical Experience in Abraham Abulafia,* trans. Jonathan Chipman (Albany, New York: SUNY Press, 1988), 179–227, for a full exposition of sexual imagery in the works of Abulafia.

7. Imbibing from Rabbi Eleazar of Worms the use of gematria and notarikon, Abulafia assumed the pen name of Raziel ("secrets of God"), which is the same sum of the Hebrew letters as in the name Abraham. He then replaces and adds letters and gets from the sum of his calculations of the name Abraham the word for *limbs* in Hebrew (*aivarim*), which is 248; this is, according to tradition, the number of positive commandments found in the Torah. Since Abraham was the reputed author of *Sefer Yetsirah,* Abulafia asserts that this is the key to the fundamentals of the Jewish faith. See Amnon Gross, ed., *M'tzaref HaSekhel v'Sefer HaOt* (Jerusalem: Aharon Barzoni and Son, 2001), http://www.hebrewbooks.org/49748; printed from manuscripts from Hebrew University.

8. See Scholem, op. cit., 146–155. Translated from a manuscript, this is an intimate description of the rapture of an anonymous student of Abulafia. It is well worth the reading for an inside account of the achievement of what Abulafia taught. See also Idel, *The Mystical Experience.*

גבורה

7 The Zohar

A more direct connection between Isaac the Blind and Azriel ben Menahem on the development of the Kabbalah took place at approximately the same time Abulafia was traveling through the lands of the Mediterranean. This connection was the publishing of a book which would take its place among the classics of Judaism alongside the Bible and the Talmud: the Zohar (Book of Radiance). In it, the previous depictions of creation flowing from the Ain Sof (Infinite God) through the Sefirot were to be given their classical reformulation.

It was Moses de Leon (1250–1305) who brought the Zohar to the attention of the world of the mystics. The reputed author is Rabbi Simeon ben Yohai, who lived in the second century BCE. However, the authorship of the Zohar has always been one that has excited scholarly discussion. Regardless of the author's identity, it does not diminish the Zohar's importance for the development of the Kabbalah. Gershom Scholem, in his classic *Major Trends in Jewish Mysticism*, devotes an entire chapter to an examination of the Zohar and the strong possibility that Moses de Leon was its author.[1]

Very much like the Bible, the Zohar is really not a book but a literature, the main part of which is a *midrash* (homily) on the Torah.[2]

Midrash is a means of commentary dating back to the Tannaitic period. It not only elucidates the plain, literal meaning of the text (*pshat*) but also draws sermonic inference from it. The Zohar uses another type of midrash, *raza* in Aramaic or *sod* in Hebrew ("secret"). Of the three great commentators on the Torah of the Middle Ages, Rashi (Rabbi Shelomo ben Yitshak, 1040–1105) used *pshat* and *drash* (homiletical) interpretations, and Abraham Ibn Ezra (1092–1170) used only *pshat* and very critical examination of the text. It was only Rabbi Moses ben Nahman (Ramban, 1094–1170) who introduced *sod*, or a mystic interpretation, as an element in his commentary.[3] While Nahmanides was sparing in his use of *sod* interpretation of the Torah, the Zohar uses it to a greater extent than in the previous commentaries.[4]

The name of the book comes from the Hebrew word for "shining" or "light" and sometimes is translated as "splendor." The word *zohar* is found in Ezekiel

8:2 and again in Daniel 12:3: "The wise ones will shine like the *radiance* of the firmament," emphasis added.

In the Merkavah mysticism of the first millennium, the mystic was content to stand before God's throne to behold His Glory. In the Kabbalah of the Zohar, we are brought into the Glory itself and are able contemplate the inner workings of God's creation as it manifests through the Sefirot. Every word in the Bible now is connected to one of the Sefirot and thus fashions its own commentary in a complete deconstruction of the text. And in contrast to the old midrash of the Tannaim, where the text never really loses its simple meaning, the more modern midrash of the Zohar contends that the *pshat* can never be the real meaning![5]

The symbolism of a tree or Adam as First Man is used to explain how the Sefirot evolve from the Ain Sof. The hidden God manifests through His creation, and this unfolding of God can be pictured only symbolically as Adam the First Man. Through the ten stages of the Sefirot in the inner world of God, He descends to reveal Himself to humanity. But the Sefirot cannot be thought of as individual stages without connection. All is connected for all is God.[6]

Keter Elyon
High Crown

Binah
"Understanding," intellect of God

Hokhmah
"Wisdom" of God

Da'at[7]
"Knowledge" of God
(combination form of *Hokhmah* and *Binah*)

Din/Gevurah
"Judgment/Severity" of God

Hesed
"Loving-kindness" of God

Rahamin/Tiferet
"Compassion/Beauty" of God
(balance of *Gevurah* and *Hesed*)

Hod
"Majesty" of God

Netsah
"Eternity"
(continuing existence of God)

Yesod
"Foundation"
(source of all of God's actions)

Malkhut-Shekhinah = ***Keneset Yisrael***
"Kingship/Immanence" of God — "Community of Israel" in its idealized state[8]

As Scholem points out, *Malkhut* usually is described in the Zohar as the *Keneset Yisrael* (Community of Israel in its idealized state) or as *Shekhinah* (Immanent Presence of God).

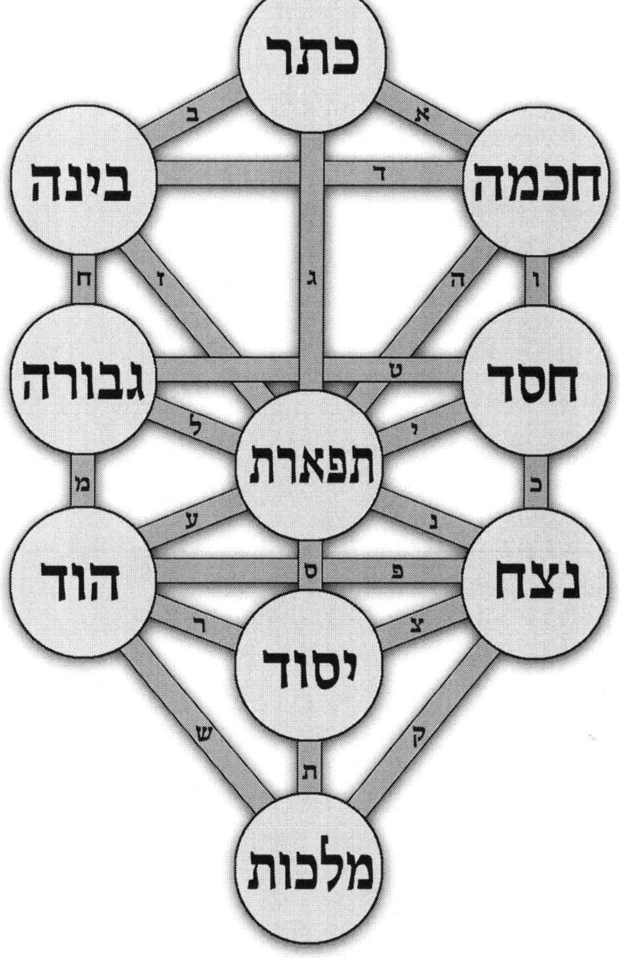

One of the most important principles of traditional Jewish thought is that God created the world out of nothing. Theologians often use the Latin term *Creatio ex Nihilo* or the Hebrew term *Yesh May-Ain*. So for the Zohar, for God to create the world, that which was Infinite in His will became Nothingness, and within this nothingness, which is the Keter Elyon, all the other stages of the Sefirot unfolded in this plan of creation.[9]

To elucidate its *Yesh May-Ain* philosophy, the Zohar begins with an exegesis of Genesis 1:1 ("'In the beginning' God created the Heavens and the earth,") taking us into the process of creation before the actual creation of the world:

> In the beginning of the will of the King [God's initial action] He engraved engravings [signs] in the pure upper regions. A dark spark proceeded from the most closed of closed spaces of the Infinite, an unformed matter affixed in a ring that was neither black nor white, nor red nor green, not any color at all. When the line of light spread, it made colors to shine. In the innermost part of the flame a well sprang and from it were colored the forms below. Hidden in the innermost of the mystery of the Infinite. The well broke but did not break through the air that surrounded it. It was not apparent at all until from the stress of its breaking through shone a point hidden on high. Beyond this point nothing is known and for this it is called "Beginning," the first saying of the King.[10]

Something had to happen in God, who is Infinite and fills all of space, to allow for creation. For traditional commentators this means that God had to withdraw those colors from around the universe to a point from which all creation flowed. The four lights are the Sefirot of Wisdom, of Understanding, of Compassion/Beauty, and of the Kingdom = Immanence. After the withdrawal from the point of concentration, creation began.[11]

In other symbolism, God is seen as creating the Primeval Adam and fashioning all creation from this being. In that section of the Zohar called "The Great Assembly," *he* [Adam] is that which includes everything from Heaven to earth. *He* is the Heavenly Crown, the Sefirah from which all creation proceeds. This neatly deflates the anthropomorphism of the Bible, for all descriptions of human attributes can be traced not to the Ain Sof but to the Primeval Adam. In earlier mysticism this was done by speaking of the Glory.[12]

The first act of visible creation fades into the background as we are brought into the workings of the Divine. The first verse of Genesis is turned on its head: "In the beginning the *Ain Sof* created God (*Elohim*)." *Elohim* is now associated with the Wisdom Sefirah, and Wisdom uses the Understanding Sefirah to create the rest of the universe. The book of Genesis begins with the words "In the beginning, Elohim created the heavens and the earth." In the book of Proverbs, "Wisdom" and "Understanding" are grouped together. And when the book of Proverbs speaks of "Wisdom" it is stated, "God has acquired me [Wisdom], the beginning of His way." Thus the interpretation is that in God's creation of the world He used wisdom as His first means.[13]

Semitic words have triconsonantal roots, and Hebrew vowels are diacritics. The noun *binah* ("understanding") has the same root (BNH) as the verb "build." Thus we might say that God used "Wisdom" as the blueprint and "Understanding" as the actual material of creation.

The fluid relationships of the Sefirot to the Infinite and each other can be likened to the circulatory system, for life force flows from top to bottom and bottom to top. The harmony of this universe was broken by Adam's sin, which caused the essence of God to retreat into transcendence, which is hidden from man. The idea of God retreating because of sin and being brought near by the fulfilling of His commandments is found in the midrash.[14]

As in the Shiur Komah, the first expression of the Divine Will is in the person of Adam Kadmon (the primeval macroanthropos) from which the Infinite can create the Finite. From primeval man came four spiritual realms:

- *Atzilut* ("Emission" = Divine Wisdom)
- *Beriah* ("Creation" = Divine Intellect)
- *Yetsirah* ("Formation" = Divine Emotions/Feelings)
- *Asiyah* ("Activation" = Divine Retaliation)[15]

The problem of *Yesh May-Ain* ("something from nothing") was solved in the minds of these kabbalists by *tzimtzumim,* "contractions" of the Divine fullness down through these realms. From stage to stage the intensity was reduced and the energy emitted created realms that transferred their own power to lower levels. We will return to this concept when we discuss the influence of Lurianic Kabbalah.

As the various books of the Zohar unfold, the Sefirot develop into *partzufim*, an Aramaic term for the Hebrew word *panim* (faces). We will return to the concept of partzufim in our later discussion of Lurianic Kabbalah.

It is in the enfolding of the last Sefirot that we meet *Yesod* (source of all of God's actions). The Zohar gives this Sefirah phallic implications and, in its interaction with *Malkhut-Shekhinah*, we have symbolic sexuality as *Yesod* flows into the last Sefirah.[16]

In the older rabbinic writings, *Shekhinah* meant nothing more than God's immanent presence. Nouns in Hebrew carry male/neuter or female gender values. In the Zohar, the feminine suffix of the word *Shekhinah* ("ah") is taken literally, endowing a female personality. So the Spanish term for this Sefirah is *Matronita* (*matron* in the Roman sense of a lady of high birth). The feminization of the *Shekhinah* is quite an astonishing feat for the Zohar to accomplish and have so many Jews accept. It almost smacks of the Roman Catholic concept that no one can come to Jesus unless he comes to Mary first. The *Matronita*, among other facts about the Zohar too numerous to mention, have led many scholars to claim its publication in thirteenth-century Spain. The most famous of all scholars of Jewish mysticism, Gershom Scholem, was convinced it was the work of a single individual, Moses de Leon of Guadalajara.[17] But no doubt about it, this conception of the

Shekhinah as the feminine part of God softened the image of God so often pictured in the Bible as a "Man of War," fighting the battles of His people. [18]

The image of that part of God as woman with all her motherly tenderness opened the door to mystical meditation. This *Raza de-Mehemanuta* ("secret of faith") is profoundly comforting to an exiled and reviled people. Queen, bride, mother . . . is this not the very image of the Mother Goddess worshipped for so many centuries in the Mediterranean world? Only the essential unity of the Sefirot and the constant admonition that all is symbolic stays the purity of the original monotheism.

The Zohar seeks to explain two of the great problems of a monotheistic faith. The first: How could an infinite God who is *HaMakom* ("the Place" in Hebrew) create the world from nothing? The second, perhaps more important and more relevant to the human condition: If God is just and loving, how did evil enter into the world and why do the wicked prosper while the righteous suffer? Rabbi Yanai (second to third century CE) gave up on this issue and said that the rabbis could find no adequate answer! [19]

The Zohar explains evil as being contained in the Sefirah of *Din* (strict "Judgment"), and in the process of the enfolding of one Sefirah into another, evil escaped from its potentiality to reality. Thus the reality of evil is an essential component and byproduct of creation. The notion that the strict judgment of God could escape in its transition from potential to actual and produce the realm of evil is not as farfetched as it might seem. [20]

The Zohar offers another explanation for evil. Adam is blamed for worshipping only the Shekhinah as the Tree of Knowledge, separating it from the worship that, at the same time, should have been offered to the Tree of Life; thus we live in a broken world and the Shekhinah and God are separated. Through study, prayer, and commandment, the religious acts of the community of Israel are the only available means to heal the breach. If Israel as a community is the Shekhinah, then by its actions it can influence the upper regions of the Sefirot. [21]

The psychological advantage this spiritual agency gives to a persecuted minority is that by the action of a saintly few, despite the bitter reality of daily life, the world will be redeemed. One can fully understand that the rational philosophy that competed with the Kabbalah for the minds of the Jewish community did not have a ghost of a chance in the hearts of the populace.

The victory of Kabbalah over rational philosophy was accomplished not only by its innate appeal but also by the successive disasters that overcame the Jewish people in the course of the Middle Ages. The Franco-German community was destroyed by the Crusades and by ensuing persecution and legal restriction. The Iberian community was destroyed a short hundred years after the appearance of the Zohar, beginning with the pogroms of 1391. Mass murder was coupled with mass conversion.

By 1497 there were no publicly professing Jews in the lands of Spain and Portugal. The year 1648 saw the terrible massacres in Poland, a land that in the hundred years prior produced some of the greatest Jewish legal minds of all time. A battered, impoverished, and persecuted people could find comfort in being ushered into the very inner sanctum in which the Divinity resides. The empowerment of the forlorn made them partners with their God in the fulfillment of creation and the perfection thereof in the final salvation. The Zohar raises the impoverished into what its reputed author Moses de Leon calls "the courtiers of the royal court." It is so much easier to make poverty a badge of honor when you are impoverished![22]

And for all of its sometime radical symbolism, the Zohar demands *devekut* (adherence) to God. This is translated into daily life by Torah study, chastity, repentance, charity, prayer, and by scrupulously following all the commandments. Thus no rabbinic officials could find fault with this, and so the Zohar never underwent the ban that was placed against Maimonides' *Guide for the Perplexed*.[23]

The Zohar brought together all the contemporary ideas about the soul before, during, and after its existence on earth. The soul is a tripartite combination modeled on the Greek philosophical division of it as it developed in the competing ideas of Plato and Aristotle and as it passed through Arab philosophers into the thought of Jewish philosophers such as Maimonides. The soul was said to be composed of *nefesh* (id), *ruah* (spirit), and *neshamah* (holy spark). It is the *neshamah* alone that, by devotion to the Kabbalah, can activate in the practitioner the soul's reunion with the *Binah* (Divine intellect) whence it came. In the Zohar, all souls are thought to be preexistent, and after death there is confusion between the doctrine of reincarnation and a belief in reward and punishment.[24]

Whether this belief in reincarnation was taken from the Cathars (Catholic heretics) of Provence or goes back to the influence of Greek Orphism on early Jewish mysticism is a subject for scholarly discussion. Regarding punishment in the Zohar, the *neshamah* leaves the deceased sinner and is replaced by a polluted spirit from the "other side." The sinner suffers the purification of the tortures of *Gehenna* (Jewish Purgatory) or, in the case of the most flagrant offender, is extinguished. As reward, the righteous are clothed in heavenly garments and enjoy the vision of bliss in Paradise.[25]

For the Zohar, the Sabbath day is special, for not only do sinners in *Gehenna* have rest from their afflictions, but also every Jew receives an extra soul for the day. It also celebrates the union of the Shekhinah with the Holy One, Blessed Be He. This part of the Zohar is found before the official call to prayer in the Sephardic liturgy and in the prayer books of those who follow the customs of Isaac Luria.[26]

In the Ashkenazic liturgy there is a reading from the Zohar right before the Torah is taken out of the ark in the Sabbath morning service, beginning:

> Blessed is Your crown and Your place. . . . For You I long, and to Your dear Holy Name I offer praise. May it be Your will that You open my heart and the hearts of all Your people Israel to Your Torah and fulfill the requests of my heart and the hearts of all Your people Israel, for goodness, for life and for peace."[27]

NOTES

1. See Scholem, *Major Trends,* 156–204.
2. Ibid., 157.
3. "Moses ben Nahman Gerondi (RaMBaN; known also as Nahmanides and Bonastruc da Porta)," *Jewish Encyclopedia,* http://www.jewishencyclopedia.com/articles/11129-moses-ben-nahman-gerondi.
4. See Scholem, op. cit., 210.
5. Ibid., 210 f.
6. Ibid., 213.
7. *Da'at* is a later addition not found in the Zohar. Luria replaces *Keter* with *Da'at.* See Adin Steinsaltz, *The Thirteen Petalled Rose* (New York: Basic Books, 1980), 39.
8. See Scholem, op. cit., 213 f.
9. Ibid., 217.
10. Ibid., 218 f. Scholem's translation is poetic. I have tried to simplify it, based on the original Aramaic. An excellent translation of the Zohar, notated with in-depth scholarship, is: Daniel C. Matt, *The Zohar* (Stanford: Stanford University Press, 2004). See also the beginning of Parashat Bereishit 1:15a.
11. See Scholem, op. cit., 215.
12. Ibid., 217.
13. Prov. 8:22.
14. Genesis Rabbah XIX:7. See Ephraim E. Urbach, *The Sages,* trans. Israel Abrahams (Cambridge: Harvard University Press, 1987).
15. For a description of the worlds by a kabbalist scholar, see Steinsaltz, *Rose,* 3–31.
16. See Scholem, op. cit., 227.
17. See Scholem, op. cit., 156–204. In this Scholem was preceded by Heinrich Graetz et al., "ZOHAR (called also in the earlier literature Midrash ha-Zohar and Midrash de-Rabbi Shim'on ben Yohai)," *Jewish Encyclopedia,* http://www.jewishencyclopedia.com/articles/15278-zohar.
18. See especially Exod. 15, which is recited daily in the morning prayers.
19. Mishnah Avot 4:19 (15).
20. See Scholem, op. cit., 235–239.
21. Ibid., 232.
22. Ibid., 234.

23. Ibid., 233 f.

24. Ibid., 240–243.

25. Ibid.

26. *Zohar II,* 135a–b in *Siddur Beit Yosef* (Vienna: Josef Shulsinger, 1922), 238 f.

27. *Zohar Shemot* (Vilna: Widow Rom and Brothers, 1894), Vaykhel, 206. In most of the prayer books of Nusach Ashkenaz, the reading is: "May it be Thy will to open my heart to Thy Torah . . . and to fulfill the desires of my heart and the heart of all Thy people Israel for good, for life and for peace. Amen." The ellipsis represents the original words found in the Zohar that are left out of the prayer book: "and grant me sons that do Thy will." http://opensiddur.org/wp-content/uploads/2010/08/Kabbalat-Shabbat-Nusa%E1%B8%A5-Ha-Ari-%E1%B8%A4aBaD.pdf.

חכמה

8 Christian Cabala

How the Kabbalah Saved the Talmud

Hard as it is to swallow, for some, Christianity is a form of Judaism. Both are biblically derived religions. It is interesting to speculate that if Christianity had not embraced so fully the philosophical traditions of Greece but had hewed more to the traditional Jewish forms of exegesis found among Paul and the early disciples of Jesus, then perhaps a Kabbalah that was Christian in form and substance might have been possible. The Augustine formulation of the Trinity as three personalities but one person ("that the Trinity is the one and only and true God, and also how the Father, the Son, and the Holy Spirit are rightly said, believed, understood, to be of one and the same substance or essence") surely reminds one of the Jewish Kabbalist defending the Sefirot by saying all are really one.[1]

Christianity and Judaism parted ways with an intense acrimony that is sometimes met when siblings quarrel over the legacy of parents. The Church's acceptance of the Hebrew Bible as Holy Scripture presented a problem in relations with the synagogue as to the interpretation of what both groups deemed to be revealed truth. As history unfolded, Christians were vexed by the non-acceptance by Jews of Jesus as Messiah and Savior. Although the Church tolerated Jewish existence in its lands, it saw the conversion of the Jews as a mission to be completed to bring about the final salvation. After all, the Jews were perfidious. They must realize who Jesus is but refuse to acknowledge a fact that was so very clear to every believing Christian. Jewish converts to Christianity became especially prized by the Church as weapons against the recalcitrant Jews who refused to accept the validity of Christian interpretation of scripture.

Justinian, Emperor of the Eastern, or Byzantine, Empire from 527 to 565 CE, set into law provisions affecting the inner spiritual life of the Jews in his domain. He forbade the building of new synagogues, conversion to Judaism, and the observance of Passover if it fell on the same day as Easter. However, his most pernicious interference in the life of the synagogue was the order that not only were the scriptural lessons on Sabbath and festivals to be translated into the vernacular, but now forbidden were the traditional homiletic lessons taught by the rabbis after scriptural reading.[2]

Soon enough, the Church prevailed upon the civil authorities to order that disputations between Jews and Christians be handled by rabbis and Christian clerics. With the Church battling the Albigensian heresy, Pope Innocent III quickly decided to restrict Jewish influence on Christian life. The decrees of the fourth Lateran Council of 1215 relating to the Jews can be looked upon as a prototype for the Nuremberg decrees of Nazi Germany. The disputations now took on the nature of a savage contest in which the Jews were doomed to lose.

One case in point: In June 1240, a disputation was organized by the Church in Paris with an apostate by the name of Nicholas Donin as its main prosecutor. The Jews were represented by four distinguished rabbis including Yehiel of Paris and Moses of Coucy. The charge was that the Talmud defamed Jesus and contained immoral sentiments and blasphemy. This charge resulted in the 1242 burning in Paris of twenty-four cartloads of the Talmud.[3]

The motivation to convert the Jews to Christianity led to an interest in the very books that the Jews held as sacred. This began in the Christian Bible itself with reference to passages in what they termed the Old Testament to be used as proof texts for their doctrine. Christians found the Kabbalah as a tempting portal through which they might achieve the conversion of the Jews and, after the writing of the Zohar, a certain later saint of the Church, Ramon Llull, used this very tool.[4] There even were a number of Jewish converts who used the Kabbalah as a tool for conversion. Iberian Marranos (Spanish and Portuguese converts, sometimes forced) added to the number of converts to Christianity who used the Kabbalah to influence their former co-religionists.

Christian Cabala reinterpreted Kabbalistic doctrine. The upper three Sefirot were the Trinity and the last seven the lower world.[5] But it was with the renewal of the quest for classical learning in the Renaissance that saw the beginnings of what could truly be called a Christian Cabala.

Giovanni Pico della Mirandola (1463–1494) was the first famous Gentile devotee and founder of the Christian Cabala. In a short life filled with an insatiable appetite for learning, Pico studied Hebrew with Elia del Medigo in Padua, became a bit conversant with Aramaic, and later added the study of Kabbalah to his scholarly repertoire. He prepared 900 theses for debate in Rome. His claim was "no science can better convince us of the divinity of Jesus Christ than magic and the Kabbalah." According to Pico, the first Sefirah Keter represented The Father; Hokhmah (Sapientia) represented Jesus (The Son, the Messiah) and Binah (Intelligentia) represented The Holy Spirit.[6] His attempt to import Kabbalah as a proof for Christian truth brought him near to the stake for heresy.[7]

The most famous of Christian cabbalists was Johannes Reuchlin (1455–1522) who was a scholar of profound influence. He was the real center of Hebrew teaching in Germany. Reuchlin studied the grammar of David Kimhi and produced his own Hebrew grammar in Latin, *De Rudimentis Hebraicis*. In Florence he was exposed to Pico della Mirandola and in Rome studied with Ovadiya Sforno, a Jewish biblical commentator. Reuchlin was thus a most serious student of Hebrew and Jewish biblical interpretation.

Like Pico, Reuchlin found in the Kabbalah a profound description of the inner workings of what occurred in God and the Sefirot as they related to creation and all existence. For him this could be the greatest defense of Christianity and the reconciliation of science with the mysteries of faith. Reuchlin expressed his Kabbalistic ideas in the books *De Verbo Mirifico* and *De Arte Cabbalistica*.

Reuchlin is remembered in Jewish history for his famous defense of the Talmud and Kabbalah against a Jewish renegade by the name of Johannes Pfefferkorn (1469–1523). In 1505, a year after being released from prison for burglary, Pfefferkorn converted to Christianity and was baptized. In 1507 he published *Der Juden Spiegel*, a diatribe against Jewish usury in which he demanded that Jews be forced to give up moneylending and attend sermons in churches. He also suggested that the Talmud be banned and destroyed, implying that it hindered Jews' conversion to Christianity. Pfefferkorn went on to accuse the Jews of wishing to kill Christians, and he advocated for the expulsion of the Jews. In 1509, Pfefferkorn obtained the Imperial German Emperor's authority to confiscate all Jewish books directed against Christianity. He asked Reuchlin's help as a jurist and expert. Reuchlin found that he had to take sides in the controversy.

In 1510, Reuchlin was appointed by the Emperor Maximillian to a commission that was to review the matter. In his answer Reuchlin divided the Jewish books into six classes, including the Bible, which all declared holy. He showed that any books openly insulting Christians were very few and that most Jews did not deem them of any value.

The remaining texts were necessary to Jewish worship and licensed by papal as well as imperial law. Others contained matter of scholarly value and interest, which ought not to be sacrificed just because they are connected with a faith other than Christianity. He proposed that the emperor should decree that for ten years there be two Hebrew chairs at every German university for which the Jews should furnish books.

Pfefferkorn and his colleagues among the Dominicans (the Christian order handling disputations) launched a vitriolic attack against Reuchlin, who soon found it necessary to defend himself against Inquisition charges. Reuchlin was joined in battle by other humanists such as Erasmus, who declared that Pfefferkorn, as a renegade Jew, was not to be trusted. After a long and bitter struggle, the forces of enlightenment prevailed, Reuchlin was vindicated, the Jews were spared, and their books of Talmud and Kabbalah were not consigned to the flames as they were in 1242 Paris. The debt of inspiration that Reuchlin owed the Kabbalah was well repaid![8]

The last Christian cabbalist to be mentioned here is Knorr von Rosenroth (1636–1689), a German Christian. As with other Christian cabbalists, von Rosenroth saw in the Kabbalah the proof of Christianity. In his opinion, Adam Kadmon (the Primeval Adam) is Jesus and the three highest Sefirot represent the Trinity. Rosenroth intended to write Latin translations of kabbalistic books.

He published the first two volumes of his *Kabbala Denudata, sive Doctrina Hebræorum Transcendentalis et Metaphysica Atque Theologia* (1677–1678). They contain parts of the Zohar and essays of Naphtali Herz, a Jewish Kabbalist. Rosenroth published two other volumes under the title *Kabbala Denudata* in 1684, containing the *Sha'ar ha-Shamayim* of Abraham Herrera and several of the writings of Isaac Luria.[9]

Christian Cabala reflects the on-again, off-again love-hate relationship between Christians and Jews and their quests for theological supremacy and doctrinal justification. In more recent times, non-Jews searching for spiritual exploration have been attracted to the Kabbalah.

NOTES

1. Saint Augustine, *On The Trinity,* trans. Arthur West Haddan, book 1, ch. 2, Logos Library, http://www.logoslibrary.org/augustine/trinity/0102.html.

See Zohar I 245a in Scholem, *Major Trends*: "Being is an Absolute Whole. For is not the organic life of the soul one and the same, although the function of the hands differs from that of the eyes, etc." Compare Adolph Harnack, *History of Dogma*, trans. Neil Buchanan (New York: Dover Publications, 1961), IV, 729.

2. "Justinian," *Jewish Encyclopedia,* http://www.jewishencyclopedia.com/articles/9097-justinian.

3. "Disputations," *Jewish Encyclopedia,* http://www.jewishencyclopedia.com/articles/5226-disputations.

4. See "The Christian Kabbalah," *Encyclopaedia Judaica* (Jerusalem: Keter Publishing House, 1978), X, 643–46.

5. Salo Wittmayer Baron, *A Social and Religious History of the Jews* (New York: Columbia University Press, 1969), III, 172–181.

6. "Giovanni Pico della Mirandola," Stanford Encyclopedia of Philosophy, http://plato.stanford.edu/entries/pico-della-mirandola/.

7. Cecil Roth, *The Jews in the Renaissance* (Philadelphia: Jewish Publication Society, 1978), 112–121.

8. Heinrich Graetz, *History of the Jews,* (Philadelphia: Jewish Publication Society, 1956), IV, 431–481.

9. "Rosenroth, Baron Von (Christian Knorr)," *Jewish Encyclopedia,* http://www.jewishencyclopedia.com/articles/12857-rosenroth-baron-von-christian-knorr.

בינה

9 The Spiritual Capital on the Mountaintop

The city of Safed in Israel is one of the four Jewish holy cities of Israel; Jerusalem, Hebron and Tiberias are the others. It occupies the highest elevation in Israel, close to three thousand feet above sea level. Sitting on the rift that runs from Turkey to Africa, Safed has seen its share of earthquakes that, along with outbreaks of plague, have decimated the population from time to time. The warm summers and cool winters make it an attractive place to visit and one of the few places in modern Israel that experience snow on a regular basis. It is not far from the Sea of Galilee, Israel's only inland freshwater lake, which empties into the Jordan River and down to the Dead Sea. Small in size, Safed is populated today by an artists' colony, Ethiopian and Russian immigrants, kabbalists and *ba'alei teshuvah* (Jews seeking return to their spiritual roots). Safed's topography, largely untouched by more modern development, can still give inspiration to mystical thoughts far more, perhaps, than can Jerusalem with its "Holy Trade."

Once I visited the cemetery where I saw the grave of Joseph Karo, author of three great compendia of Jewish law (halakhah) and the grave of him who is called "The Holy Lion": Ha'AR"I (The Godly Rabbi Isaac) HaKodesh (The Holy) Rabbi Isaac Luria. Their graves were piled high with prayers of petitioners who placed their written requests under stones on top of the graves so that the wind would not blow away the papers. In the bases of the upright headstones, compartments were hollowed out so the devout could light candles and place them within, safe from the elements that might extinguish them.

The day was sunny, but a strong cold breeze whipped around the mountaintop, and I stood on an outcrop and looked down on the mikvah (ritual bath) where Ha'AR"I and the kabbalists would bathe before the Sabbath. I remember to this day the chill I felt as I stood near the grave of Ha'AR"I and looked upon the valley below. I was grasped by a feeling that, while not quite dread, was a feeling of "the other." It is difficult to describe but somewhat like the knowledge that someone is watching you whom you cannot see but you know is there. What Rudolf Otto in *The Idea of the Holy* calls the Mysterium Tremendum: the awareness of one's humanity in the face of a spiritual force beyond one's comprehension.

There, to this mikvah, according to the story, the kabbalists would go out in white garments to meet the Sabbath Bride. This custom goes back to Rabbi Haninah, who would speak of welcoming the Sabbath as Queen and Bride, and to Rabbi Yannai, who would don his prayer shawl and go out exclaiming "Come O Bride, come O Bride."[1] In the midrash, commenting on Genesis 2:3 "God blessed the Sabbath day and made it holy," Rabbi Shimon ben Yohai is quoted as saying: "The Sabbath said before The Holy One Blessed Be He: 'Master of The World, all of the others have a mate [i.e., days being paired 1-2, 3-4, 5-6] and I do not have a mate.' The Holy One Blessed Be He said to her [the Sabbath], 'Keneset Yisrael [the Community of Israel] will be your mate.' And when Israel stood before Mount Sinai, The Holy One Blessed Be He said to them: 'Remember the matter—Remember the Sabbath to betroth her (Exodus 20:8).'"[2]

In Safed, the Shekhinah was visualized as the mystical bride of God, and the Sabbath became Israel's celebration of "the marriage of the King and Queen."[3] From that time forward the introduction to the Friday evening service consists of a selection of kabbalists' Psalms and is known as Kabbalat Shabbat. Still today, across the world on Friday evenings, the doors of synagogues are opened for the last refrain of the hymn "L'kha Dodi": "Come Beloved Friend to greet the Bride, Let us receive the Shabbat."[4] That hymn was composed by Rabbi Shelomoh HaLevi Alkabetz—whose Hebrew name appears as an acrostic in its verses—from the mystic setting of Safed, the mountain capital of Kabbalah.

And it was in Safed that Alkabetz introduced his brother-in-law, Moses ben Jacob Cordovero (1522–1570), to the study of the Kabbalah. Cordovero, a brilliant Talmudist and adept in philosophy, would systemize kabbalistic thought up to his time in his first book, *Pardes Rimonim* (Pomegranate Orchard). His second work, an encyclopedia of commentary on the literature of the Zohar, *Or Yakar* (Precious Light), was sixteen volumes in length.[5]

He wrote an ethical work, *Tomer Devorah* (The Palm Tree of Deborah) that was infused with his outlook as shaped by the Kabbalah. In it, Cordovero asserts that Israel and God are bound by family ties that cannot be broken even if Israel is estranged from God because of their transgressions. I give as illustration a selection from *Tomer Devorah* to provide a small and hopefully digestible taste of his writing.

> For Behold The Holy One Blessed Be He acts with Israel in this fashion saying: "What can I do to Israel since they are my relatives; there is consanguinity between us [literally, we share the same flesh!]? For they are the daughter of the Holy One Blessed Be He and He calls her [Israel]: my daughter, my sister, my mother as the rabbis of blessed memory interpreted" [Song of Songs 3:25 where these terms occur]. And it is written: "Israel is the people who are family to Him." [Psalms 148:14] Real familial ties I have with them.

> And they are His children and thus "To the remnant [can be interpreted as flesh by a stretch of the meaning of the Hebrew] of His inheritance" that is the language of closeness of flesh [family] and finally they are His inheritance. And what does He say, "If I punish them behold the pain is Mine." As it is written [Isaiah 63:9] "In all of their sorrow it was sorrow to Him."

In this verse from Isaiah, the word "to Him" is written with "lamed-alef" which has the meaning of *no* but it is read as "lamed-vav" meaning *to Him*. Now, the letter "lamed" means *to*, so Cordovero deconstructs the text:

> It is written with "alef" to say that their sorrow reaches to highest Sefirah (Keter Elyon).

Cordovero, influenced as he was by Maimonides and medieval philosophy, conceived of a chain by which the flow of the Ain Sof descended into the lower Sefirot.

Thus, starting with Adam Kadmon, the repository of the Divine Wisdom, the Sefirot and the Four Spiritual realms of *Azilut* (Emission), *Beriah* (Creation), *Yetsirah* (Formation), and *Asiyah* (Activation) enfolded one down through the other. Thus Cordovero imagined the trickle-down flow of Divinity into the lowest realms of existence.[6]

As profound an influence as Cordovero was on the systemization of the Kabbalah, he was soon eclipsed by a student who appeared in Safed a mere two years before Cordovero's death. Isaac ben Solomon Luria was born (1534–1572) to an Ashkenazic (German) father and Sephardic (Spanish) mother. His father died when he was quite young, but a rich maternal uncle supported him and had him study under the outstanding rabbis of Egypt, Rabbi David ibn Zimra and Rabbi Betzaleil Ashkenazi (himself an author of a compendium of commentary on several tractates of the Talmud known as *Shittah Mekubetzet*). Luria proved adept in his studies, but after marriage he took to a hermitic life of week-long meditation and only returned to his family for the Sabbath. In 1569 he settled in Safed and became a student of Cordovero shortly before the latter's death. Luria was one of those few gifted charismatic leaders who, by his true sincerity, erudition, modesty and spirituality, crafted a following that was to have the most profound effect on Jewish spiritual life and that has not been equaled since Moses and the prophets of old. His teachings were transmitted by his students. Among the most important of those was Rabbi Hayyim Vital (1543–1620), who was born in Safed and who recorded much of his master's teachings. After Vital's death his writings spread, having a "powerful impact on various circles throughout the Jewish world." The works were published as *Shemonah Sh'arim* (Eight Gates) and in other forms as *Etz Hayyim* (Tree of Life) and *P'ri Etz Hayyim* (Fruit of the Tree of Life).[7]

Of Luria's own writings, there are three hymns in Aramaic to be sung at the three meals designated for the Sabbath: Shabbat evening, lunch, and the third meal. The hymn for the third meal, eaten as the Sabbath moves towards its end, is an especially popular one as this meal usually is shared with others after the Sabbath afternoon prayer. It is called "Bnei Heikhala" (Courtiers of the Palace):

> O courtiers of the palace, who yearn to see the splendor of Z'eir Anpin [The Impatient One]: Be present at this meal at which the King has engraved His signs. Be happy, rejoice in this gathering together with the angels and all heavenly beings; Rejoice now, at this most appropriate time, when there is no sadness.
>
> Draw near to Me, behold My strength, for there are no harsh judgments.
> They are cast out, they may not enter, these arrogant dogs [evil forces].
> I invite the "Ancient of Days" at this auspicious time, and all [impure powers] will be surely removed.
>
> It is His revealed will to annul all the powers of impurity; He will hurl them into their abysses and He will hide them in the clefts of the rocks.
> For this time of Minhah is a time of joy for Z'eir Anpin.[8]

Remember that the Zohar affirms that every Jew has an extra soul for the Sabbath, and even the punished souls in *Gehenna* (Purgatory) receive time off from their punishment on the Sabbath day.

Luria was not satisfied with Cordovero's chain of creation from the Ain Sof. If there was a chain from one stage to the other, how could there be any finite existence? Would not the quality of the Or Ain Sof (Light of the Infinite) prohibit any independent existence? If God is infinite, how can anything else come into existence? So Luria came up with the most radical exposition of how creation of the finite from the Infinite was possible, and this was the doctrine of *Tzimtzum* (Contraction).[9]

According to the doctrine of Tzimtzum, at the center of the Ain Sof there was a contraction of the Divine in order for creation to take place. This created an empty space but the space was not completely empty, for there was a residue (Reshimu) that remained, similar to oil that clings to a jar even after most of it has been poured out. In the empty space there appeared a new one-directional light which became the source of all new creation; this is Adam Kadmon (Primeval Man). From the orifices of his head, the lights of the Sefirot came into being. At first there was no differentiation between the Sefirot. Special vessels were created to contain the lights. The three highest Sefirot had vessels that contained their lights. But for the lower six Sefirot, when it came their turn to be contained in the vessels, the light was too powerful and it broke the vessels. This "breaking of the vessels" is called *Shevirat HaKelim*. In a midrash called *B'raishit Rabbah* ("The Great Midrash"), there is a statement from Rabbi Abahu that God created and destroyed worlds until He settled on this one.[10]

But Shevirat HaKelim is a very important point in Luria's conception of how evil came into the world.[11] The forces of evil are called the *Kelipot* (shells/ husks); they existed in the Reshimu, before the breaking of the vessels. The cleansing of the Sefirot of the Kelipot was brought about by the breaking of the vessels, but that gave a real existence to evil in the world as lights were no longer contained in the Reshimu but now gained reality in an independent existence. Referring to the Zohar's comments on Genesis 36:31—"And these are the Kings that reigned in the land of Edom" (in which Edom refers to stern judgment)—Luria has evil and its demonic forces now arise as the "Klipah from the rubbish of these destroyed" primordial kings.[12] Notice how Luria explains how creation proceeds from the Infinite and at the same time how evil came into its real existence. The damage from the Shevirat HaKelim has caused evil to find its way into all of the creative life processes. The divine elements are now mixed with the evil elements in the world. And now we come to one of the most powerful of Luria's ideas and that is *Tikkun* (Rectification).[13]

According to Luria interpreting Genesis 1:27, "God created man in His own image, in the image of God He created him, male and female He created them"; this refers to the form of the Sefirot in Adam Kadmon.[14] Just as body and soul in man act together, so too in Adam Kadmon the Sefirot are in harmony but their form remains only in potential. Five lights (eyes, ears, nose, mouth and forehead) proceeded from Adam Kadmon and interacted with each other to produce "the world of chaos."[15]

This is a stage in the emergence of the Sefirot before the world of *Atzilut* (Emission), the first of the four worlds conceived by Cordovero.[16] As the Sefirot came into being in the vessels that contained them, they were ten independent *Iggulim* (Circles) without any relationship to each other. Since the Tzimtzum was an equal withdrawal on all sides, the result was circular in shape; the light that entered it thereafter was both circular and unilinear.[17] This was the world of *Tohu* (Chaos), or the weak light of the vessels acting independently.

As the Divine light poured into the vessels of the Sefirot of Keter (Crown) and Hokhmah (Divine Wisdom), these vessels could contain the Divine light because of their closeness to the source. But as the Divine light entered into the Sefirah of Binah (Divine Understanding) down to Yesod (Foundation), there occurred the Shevirat HaKelim. However, the final Sefirah—Malkhut-Shekhinah—remained partially intact (perhaps the force of the break had been partially spent by Divine decree) but is exiled. The representation of this exile is Keneset Israel (Community of Israel). The exile of the Shekhinah is first mentioned in the Mekhilta of Rabbi Ishmael, referring to the presence of God going into exile with Israel.[18]

The remnants of the broken vessels fell into the Tohu, becoming innumerable fragments each animated by *Nitzuzot* (Sparks) of their original light. The sparks that contained Divine light were accepted back into the higher realms but those that did not ascend fell and produced the Kelipot; that is, they fell into the realm of impurity and evil.[19] (This is connected by interpretation with Genesis 36:31. Edom represents judgment untempered by compassion.[20] The effect of the process is to liberate evil from its suppression in the realm of Strict Judgment, but that liberation will make possible evil's final removal through Tikkun.)

The four spiritual worlds of Creation for Luria begin with the region of Tikkun. It is first achieved where the Sefirot interact with each other so each of the ten includes the others as a latent force within it. The Tikkun is completed in the world of Atzilut after Shevirat HaKelim, by the Sefirot becoming partzufim (Divine Faces). That which was expounded first in the Zohar becomes with Luria a system in which six primary partzufim are divided into twelve secondary forms.

The partzufim are personified. From Sefirah Keter comes *Atik Yomin* ("Ancient of Days," the inner will from God the Infinite) and *Arikh Anpin* ("Patient One," source of Divine love in the Sefirah of Keter).

Hokhmah is Abba ("Father," source of intellect) on the right side while Binah is Ima ("Mother," intellectual understanding producing pregnant emotions) on the left side of the schema.

Father and Mother produce *Zeir Anpin* ("Impatient One," with six Sefirot that represent emotions born of Mother) on the left side and finally *Nukvah* ("Female," daughter seeking companionship with Zeir Anpin). Thus the Shekhinah will be reunited and all will be *shaleim*—complete—which has the same Hebrew root as *shalom* (peace).

By the partzufim acting in *Yosher* (uprightness) as a human's body and soul act together, the lack of harmony that started the Shevirat HaKelim is restored. The world of Atzilut, which is the world of Divine unity, has all its sparks from the Tohu restored completely.

However, for the lower worlds of Beriah, Yetsirah and Asiyah, since they are further removed from the world of Atzilut, their correction can only be achieved from below. The process by which God conceives Himself and creates the world cannot reach its final conclusion in God. It is man who must finish the work of the King by restoring the kingdom to Him.[21]

According to Luria, Shevirat HaKelim was a necessary condition for evil to enter the world so man could be rewarded or punished according to his deeds.

All future souls were actually in Adam who, with Eve, when they were in the Garden of Eden, were actually in the world of Yetsirah and the high Sefirah of

Tiferet. They were to correct and gather the exiled sparks of holiness in the lower spiritual worlds.

As to the soul itself, Luria held that from five partzufim were emitted five souls. In ascending order:

Nefesh (breath of life) In ancient times, this was always the lowest in any order. It is derived from the *Akkadian Napishtum* (throat/gullet) as in Psalms 69:2: "waters have come up to my neck."

Ruah (spirit/wind)

Neshamah (soul)

Havah (life) The name *Eve* is *Havah* in Hebrew, the mother of all living things.

Yehidah (singular) This is the highest soul whose source is in the Sefirah of Keter (Crown) in the world of Azilut, associated with the Messiah.[22]

All of these souls were created with Adam, and they are matched with Adam's organs so there are souls of higher and lower rank. Adam's sin caused all the souls to be confused in one another so that even the purest souls have elements of the Kelipot. Because of this, all have the Yetser HaRa, the evil impulse described by the rabbis of the Mishnah. Once the Messiah comes, the impulse to do evil will be destroyed.[23]

Luria not only believed in the doctrine of *gilgul neshamah* (reincarnation) but posited that this reincarnation happened not only in the bodies of humans and animals but could also be in inanimate objects, even in stones. To reincarnation he added the theory of *ibbur* (impregnation), whereby the soul of a dead person could be attached to the soul of a living human.[24]

The sin of Adam and Eve demoted the souls to the world of Asiyah. Now it is incumbent upon every Jew to redeem the Holy Sparks from the realm of the Kelipot. This is done by special attention shown to the performance of every mitzvah, even those mitzvot that, at face value, may seem the most inconsequential.[25]

This places a heavy responsibility on the individual, but it is also unbelievably empowering. Imagine yourself a poor, persecuted person of perhaps even modest intellectual attainment. You learn, however, that by performing a mitzvah with the proper intention you have the ability to bring about salvation by the renewal of what was in the beginning of creation, i.e., the Holy Sparks. The proper intention was spelled out for you in a *Kavanah* (Intention) that stated a purpose of cosmic importance for your performance.[26]

This is seen so clearly in the performance of the commandment of *Sefirat HaOmer* (counting the Omer). In Biblical days, the Jews were commanded

(Leviticus 23:10–16) to bring a sheaf from the new barley harvest to the Temple after the holiday of Passover. They were then to count from that time fifty days until the holiday of Shavuot.[27] After the destruction of the Second Temple, the practice of bringing the new sheaf was discontinued but the counting gained new significance. Accordingly when counting the Omer (the days between Passover and Shavuot), the following is said every night, according to Lurianic custom:

> To bring about the unification of the Holy One Blessed Be He and His Shekhinah [as if conducting the Sacred Marriage!] with fear and love to unite the name YH with VH [symbolically God's name is cut asunder and by the sacred union it is restored] in a perfect union in the name of all Israel behold I am ready and prepared to fulfill the positive commandment of counting the Omer as it is written in the Torah: "And you shall count from the morrow of the Sabbath from the day of your bringing the sheaf of waving [the priest performed this in the Temple] it will be seven complete weeks until the morrow of the seventh Shabbat [week] you will count fifty days and bring a new grain offering to God." Let Your graciousness, O Lord our God, be upon us; and establish the work of our hands upon us, the work of our hands establish it.[28]

The blessing is then pronounced and the number of the day is proclaimed.

The counting takes on a mystical purification as a husband would wait for his wife, counting the days from her menses to her purification in the mikveh, after which he may be joined to her in cohabitation.[29] So, all Israel must count each day in expectation of being joined to God with the giving of the Torah on the holiday of Shavuot.[30]

But each day has a *Sod*, or mystical interpretation, attached to it (see chart, p. 65). For each week is under the influence of a different Sefirah. Thus the first week is under the Sefirah of Hesed (God's love). According to Lurianic Kabbalah, each of the Sefirot has within it an inclusion of all the other Sefirot; for example, the first day's *Sod* is Hesed that is within Hesed. The next day's Sod is Gevurah (strength) and that is also within Hesed. For the seven weeks, as the Omer is counted in the evening, each week has a specific Sefirah and each day of that week is apportioned a different Sefirah, from Hesed until Malkhut. The last day for the completion of the count is Malkhut that itself is within Malkhut, and so the fullness of the Shekhinah is brought about with the celebration of the holiday of the Giving of the Torah on the morrow. Thus, the counting brings about a perfect rectification.[31]

So the custom of a Tikkun Leil Shavuot (Rectification for the night of Shavuot) became a time to stay up the whole night of the holiday studying religious selections.[32]

WEEK NUMBER	SEFIRAH	ATTRIBUTE	ANCESTOR
1	Hesed	loving-kindness	Abraham
2	Gevurah	judgment/severity	Isaac
3	Tiferet	compassion/beauty	Jacob
4	Netsah	eternity	Moses
5	Hod	majesty	Aaron
6	Yesod	foundation	Joseph
7	Malkhut	kingship/immanence	David

1 Hesed of Hesed	2 Gevurah of Hesed	3 Tiferet of Hesed	4 Netsah of Hesed	5 Hod of Hesed	6 Yesod of Hesed	7 Malkhut of Hesed
8 Hesed of Gevurah	9 Gevurah of Gevurah	10 Tiferet of Gevurah	11 Netsah of Gevurah	12 Hod of Gevurah	13 Yesod of Gevurah	14 Malkhut of Gevurah
15 Hesed of Tiferet	16 Gevurah of Tiferet	17 Tiferet of Tiferet	18 Netsah of Tiferet	19 Hod of Tiferet	20 Yesod of Tiferet	21 Malkhut of Tiferet
22 Hesed of Netsah	23 Gevurah of Netsah	24 Tiferet of Netsah	25 Netsah of Netsah	26 Hod of Netsah	27 Yesod of Netsah	28 Malkhut of Netsah
29 Hesed of Hod	30 Gevurah of Hod	31 Tiferet of Hod	32 Netsah of Hod	33 Hod of Hod	34 Yesod of Hod	35 Malkhut of Hod
36 Hesed of Yesod	37 Gevurah of Yesod	38 Tiferet of Yesod	39 Netsah of Yesod	40 Hod of Yesod	41 Yesod of Yesod	42 Malkhut of Yesod
43 Hesed of Malkhut	44 Gevurah of Malkhut	45 Tiferet of Malkhut	46 Netsah of Malkhut	47 Hod of Malkhut	48 Yesod of Malkhut	49 Malkhut of Malkhut

Much has been made by some of the influence of Lurianic Kabbalah on the success of Sabbatai Sevi (1626–1676) and his prophet Nathan of Gaza in the messianic movement that they founded.[33] However, analysis of the situation of Jews in the seventeenth century will lead to the conclusion that Lurianic Kabbalah may have been used by Nathan of Gaza to buttress his claims for Sabbatai Sevi, but it was not the compelling reason for so many to follow Sevi and Nathan.

The year 1666 was looked to across the Christian world for the arrival of the Messiah or, as Christians called it, the Second Coming. In England, the Fifth Monarchy movement stirred men of both high and low decree. In an interpretation of The Book of Revelation, the number 666 was associated with the defeat of the forces of evil.[34] The year 1648 saw the decimation of the largest Jewish community in the world—that of Poland—by the Cossacks and Tartars under Bogdan Khemilnitsky.[35] The Jewish soul in the seventeenth century was exhausted and longed for relief. The printing press allowed for the publication and dissemination of all sorts of tracts that could attribute miracles to Sevi which would only be disproved weeks after their damage had been done. In 1666, given the choice between martyrdom and conversion to Islam, this would-be messiah chose the turban over the headsman and so vanished from Jewish communal life, leaving in his wake a new sect (Donmeh) who followed his example.[36]

Despite the misappropriation of Lurianic Kabbalah by Sabbatai Sevi and any self-proclaimed messiah thereafter, this manifestation of Jewish mysticism has remained a potent force in Jewish religious life.

For Luria, the *galut* (exile) of the Jews is not a catastrophe. Instead, this exile has for its goal the salvation of all the souls of the human race and will fulfill the prophecy of Israel being an *Or L'Goyim* (a light unto the nations).[37]

We will see in the following pages how the Kabbalah of Ha'AR"I helped shape a burst of spiritual energy in lands wracked by poverty and persecution.

NOTES

1. Bava Kamma 32b.
2. B'raishit Rabbah 11:8. The Hebrew verb *kadesh* means "to sanctify" and also "to betroth."
3. Gershom Scholem, *Kabbalah* (New York: Dorset Press, 1987), 195.
4. *Ha-Siddur Ha-Shalem, The Daily Prayer Book*, ed. Philip Birnbaum (New York: Hebrew Publishing Company, 1949), 243–247. See the Chabad website for customs relating to Sabbath eve: http://www.chabad.org/library/article_cdo/aid/1046922/jewish/Why-do-we-turn-around-on-Friday-nights.htm.
5. "Moses ben Jacob Cordovero," *Jewish Encyclopedia*, http://www.jewishencyclopedia.com/articles/12672-remak-moses-ben-jacob-cordovero.
6. *Encyclopaedia Judaica* (Jerusalem: Keter Publishing House, 1971), V, 967–970.
7. Scholem, *Major Trends*, 251–255.
8. *Siddur Brakhot V'Hodaot, Nusah Ashkenaz* (New York: Hebrew Publishing Co.), 243 f.
9. Scholem, op. cit., 260–264.
10. Genesis Rabbah IX:2; see Ephraim E. Urbach, *The Sages*, trans. Israel Abrahms (Cambridge: Harvard University Press, 1987), 51–52.
11. Scholem, *Major Trends*, 265–268; *Kabbalah*, 140–144.
12. Scholem, *Major Trends*, 265 f.
13. Ibid., 273–276.
14. Ibid., 265 f.
15. Scholem, *Kabbalah*, 138.
16. Scholem, *Major Trends*, 272; 413 note 85. Cordovero introduced the concept of four worlds, though it is not found in the major part of the Zohar.
17. Scholem, *Kabbalah*, 131.
18. Referring to the presence of God going into exile with Israel, see Urbach, *The Sages*, 43.
19. Scholem, op. cit., 139.

20. Scholem, *Major Trends*, 266; *Kabbalah*, 138 f.

21. Scholem, *Major Trends*, 269–273.

22. Scholem, *Kabbalah*, 157 f.

23. Scholem, *Major Trends*, 279.

24. Ibid., 281–284. The idea of a *dybbuk*—a soul attached to another human—is portrayed masterfully in one of the most gripping of Yiddish stories "The Dybbuk," a play by S. Ansky.

25. Scholem, *Major Trends*, 274.

26. Ibid., 275–278.

27. Passover is the time of the going out from Egypt, and Shavuot is the time when Moses received the Ten Commandments on Sinai.

28. *Siddur Oholei Sheim* (Jerusalem: Hebrew Publishing Company, 2007), 197.

29. Lev. 15:19-24. On the prohibition of marital relations during the menstrual cycle, see Mishnah Niddah, Talmud and Codes therein.

30. Calendar for Sefirat HaOmer, http://hebrewbooks.org/pdfpager.aspx?req3989&st=&pgnum=1.

31. As early as the time of the Mishnah, the giving of the Torah on Mount Sinai was seen as erasing the stigma of slavery with the gift of freedom. Rabbi Yehoshua ben Levi is quoted as saying, "Do not read 'graven' on the tablets [of the Ten Commandments], but read 'freedom' on the tablets." Exod. 32:16; the same Hebrew consonants can be read as "graven" or, by substituting different vowels, "freedom." See Pirkei Avot 6:2, http://www.daat.ac.il/daat/toshba/avot/6-2.htm.

32. For the counting of the Omer, see *Siddur HaShaleim, Ashkenaz* (Jerusalem: Zundel Krauzer, 2007), 290–294. For Tikkun on the eves of Shavuot and Hoshanah Rabbah, see *Tikkunei Yesharim* (Lemberg: Hayyah Hirtz, 1837). This publisher is the wife of R. Naftali Hirtz.

33. See Gershom Scholem, *Sabbatai Sevi, The Mystical Messiah*, trans. R.J. Zwi Werblowsky (Princeton: Princeton University Press, 1973), Bollingen Series XCIII.

34. See Louise Fargo Brown, *The Political Activities of the Baptists and the Fifth Monarchy Men in England During the Interregnum* (London: Oxford University Press, 1912).

35. For the decline of Polish Jewry, see Simon M. Dubnow, *History of the Jews in Russia and Poland*, trans. I. Friedlander (New York: Ktav Publishing House, 1975), Vol. I.

36. For the Donmeh see Scholem, *Sabbatai Sevi*, and "Dönmeh," *Jewish Encyclopedia*, http://www.jewishencyclopedia.com/articles/5278-donmeh.

37. Scholem, *Major Trends*, 284.

כתר

10 Hasidism

Revolt against the Eastern Wall

From early Talmudic times, Jewish society was governed by an elite consisting of the wealthy who married into the rabbinic learning class. These leaders maintained the community and oversaw the collecting of taxes as they interfaced with the Gentile governments. To a certain degree, the Jews functioned as a state within a state, as they were allowed a degree of autonomy, especially in religious law and life as it pertained to family concerns and rites of passage.

After decades of persecution—from the Crusades (beginning in 1096) through the massacres accompanying the Black Death—Jewish life drifted from the Frankish and German lands east to Poland. The zenith of Polish Jewish life was achieved in the sixteenth century. Famous scholars whose works populate the pages of the present editions of the Talmud established and were the products of famous yeshivot (academies of rabbinical study) of Poland. The Jews were governed by the Council of the Four Lands, which gave them semi-autonomy as codified by the charter of Sigismund Augustus of August 13, 1551.

The socioeconomic condition of the Jews in what is now Poland, Lithuania, and Ukraine was at its lowest position at the dawn of the eighteenth century. The massacres of Khmelnitsky in 1648 not only left widows and orphans but destroyed the economic basis of Jewish life. This was followed quickly by the Swedish invasion in the mid-1600s and the partitioning of Poland in the 1700s. The greater portion of Polish Jewry found itself restricted to what was called The Pale of Settlement, which was in western Tsarist Russia. Jewish autonomy and freedom from persecution under the Russian Tsars fluctuated almost always to the Jews' detriment.[1]

Since the destruction of the Second Temple, synagogues were oriented to face towards Jerusalem for prayer. As the Jewish communities were established in Western Europe, synagogues were oriented to the east. This practice continued even as Jews moved into Poland.[2]

In Eastern Europe, the Jewish upper class was distinguished in the synagogues by the seats they held near the eastern wall. This is where scholars and those connected to them had the place of honor. This elite was known by the Yiddish expression, *shayne layt* (beautiful people). Beneath this group was a small middl class of craftsmen and *baalbatim* (householders); at the bottom were the *proste la*y (a phrase for the common folk that carried with it a boorish, ignorant, and vulga connotation). The overwhelming masses belonged to the lowest rung of society, those who were oppressed by persecution, unable to buy their way out of pogrom, and often dependent on charity to survive. They also were looked down upon as illiterate by the elite who, in concert with the Gentile authorities, controlled their lives. [3]

As the byword of rabbinical Judaism was "Torah study above all else," these poor folk did not even have the comfort that religion usually offers the most unfortunate of society. And Torah study meant knowledge of the Talmud and its many commentaries.

It was in the eighteenth and nineteenth centuries that the socio-spiritual revolution of Hasidism shook the Jewish world. This new form of Jewish spiritual expression was related only by name to the German Jewish Hasidism of the thirteenth century. Like it, however, was its emphasis on personal spirituality rather than intellectual acumen and understanding of rabbinic texts. Properly speaking, although mysticism and its study play a significant role in the Hasidic movement, Kabbalah was not the guiding principle of the movement's founder, Israel ben Eliezer of Mezhbizh (d. 1760). The success of Hasidism in Eastern Europe was due to his charisma and loving-kindness. Israel ben Eliezer was known as the Baal Shem Tov (Master of the Good Name) and went by the acronym, Besht. Orphaned at an early age, he was not a great scholar and earned his livelihood as a *behelfer* (Jewish educational assistant). He walked his students to and from school, and his personality endeared him to all.[4]

Like other mystics and religious founders, the Besht spent much of his time in contemplation of nature. He lived among the peasants and farmers, close to the soil. He acquired knowledge of folk remedies and was a faith healer. The Besht was a "master" of invoking the "good name" of God, that being the proper four-letter Hebrew name of God, which the Besht used to perform wondrous acts. I have in my possession a *kamea* (amulet) ascribed to the Besht. It was to be hung in the lying-in chamber of an expectant mother to ward off the evil demon Lilith, so she could not kill the newborn.[5] The Besht established himself in Mezrich and there was surrounded by many disciples, including Dov Baer, also known as the Maggid (preacher) of Mezrich, who expounded the doctrines of his master.[6]

The Besht conceived a theory that God contains all and all is encompassed by God. Creation was not a past event but rather an ongoing process. Most importantly, although never denying any of the postulates of the Judaism of his day, the Besht insisted that true spirituality was *devekut* (cleaving to God), which could be achieved through earnest prayer and performing all of one's actions with God in mind. I remember the story of a Hasid who, traveling with a companion, came to a desolate corner in a midwestern town in the United States. The Hasid took an apple and with a loud voice recited the blessing on eating from the fruit of a tree. When asked by his companion why he did such an act, the Hasid replied: "I believe no one has ever blessed God's name in this spot so I recited a blessing to bring holiness to this place."

Even sinners are not bereft of God and can be elevated to His service. As one famous story attributed to the Besht goes, upon seeing a student engrossed in a folio page of Talmud, the Besht remarked that he is so directed to the text that he has forgotten there is a God.[7]

The Besht, by reason of his charisma and genuine love of even the poorest and ignorant of Jews, became the founder of a new spiritual direction in Judaism. The success of his Hasidic movement was based on the revolution it undertook against the "occupants" of the eastern wall. No longer were the wealthiest and the learned the elite of the Jewish community. It was now the charismatic spiritualist who was inspirational.[8] No matter how impoverished, no matter how ignorant, even if the only thing you could do with the intention of serving God was to recite the Hebrew alphabet, you were on a higher level than one carrying books as an ass does, the lessons of loving God having not yet entered his heart.

This departure from elitism combined with love of the poor and oppressed Jews made it possible within a very few generations for Hasidism to become the dominant force in Eastern Europe. A new form of religious leadership was established among the Hasidim. No longer was the mastery of texts the requirement for eminence. Rather, the charismatic and spiritual appeal of the leader now known as a *Rebbe* gained prominence in contradistinction to the halakhic authority, the Rav. The Hasidic Rebbe was seen as a *tzadik* (righteous one), who bestowed on his followers the influence of Heaven to achieve their Divine mission and goal. Soon enough, the Rebbe gave his influence as an inheritance to his descendants, who then engendered separate dynasties as this consecration was handed down through the generations.

The Berditchever Rebbe, Levi Isaac, was a Hasidic master known for his tremendous acceptance and respect of the common folk, even sinners. Here is a story attributed to him:

> It was the end of Yom Kippur and, as was the custom, a poor tailor was allowed to ascend the pulpit and lead the closing prayers for this most solemn day. Before beginning as the officiant, the tailor offered up his own prayer: "You [God] wish me to repent of my sins, but I have committed only minor offenses. I may have kept leftover cloth, or I may have eaten in a non-Jewish home where I worked, without washing my hands. But Thou, O Lord, hast

committed grievous sins; Thou hast taken away babies from their mothers and mothers from their babies. Let us be quits: mayest Thou forgive me, and I will forgive Thee."

He then proceeded to officiate. After Yom Kippur the Berditchever called over the tailor and asked him to repeat what he said. After hearing him the Rebbe Levi Isaac of Berditchev scolded the tailor: "Why did you let God off so easily? You might have forced Him to redeem all of Israel."[9]

Storytelling has been appropriated as an instructional tool throughout Jewish history. In the Mishnah of former times, stories illustrated legal rulings. Now in Hasidic hands, the story was told to teach a moral lesson. It is a *vert* (word) of Torah not in the abstract, but touching the heart and soul of the people.[10]

At the tish (table, gathering), the Rebbe's followers sang *nigunim* (wordless songs) as alcohol flowed generously. The Rebbe would say a blessing before eating something and then distribute the remnants to his followers, who would be anointed by their closeness to the Rebbe's blessing.[11]

Shneur Zalman of Lyady (1745–1812), the founder of the Chabad (later known as Lubavitch) sect of Hasidism, saw the role of the tzadik not as a miracle worker but as a teacher.[12] Following the suggestion of DovBer (the Magid of Mezeritch, d. 1772), Shneur Zalman edited a new version of the *Shulhan Arukh.* This became the authoritative code for the Hasidic interpretation of Jewish law.[13]

Shneur Zalman amplified his views in the seminal text, *Collection of Sayings,* popularly referred to as *Tanya* (the first word of this work using a Talmudic term to quote from a rabbinical source from the time of the Mishnah, c. 200 CE). This work, first published in 1797, has been reprinted many times and has become the most widely disseminated text of the entire Hasidic movement.

Zalman's summary of Kabbalah used as its motto the first three emanations according to the later representation of the Sefirot: Hokhmah, Binah, Da'at (Wisdom, Understanding, Knowledge). Their acronym (ChaBaD) became the name of his movement. Clearly the choice of the first three Sefirot emphasized the intellectual over the emotional direction of Zalman and the group he founded.[14]

He emphasized meditation as an intellectual activity that was a stage above the heartfelt emotional ecstasy of other Hasidic groups. Shneur Zalman delineated a plan of action for the ordinary Jew to achieve righteousness even if he could not aspire to the level of tzadik. The everyday Jew, by following the commandments and overcoming temptations, could achieve heavenly reward.[15]

In the Tanya, Shneur Zalman wrote of the conflict that "the Godly Soul"—that comes from God—must wage against the "Soul of Flesh and Blood"—that comes from the "Shards" and the "Other Side" forces of evil that were generated in Creation, according to Lurianic Kabbalah.

For Zalman, the souls of the Gentiles come completely from the realm of "Other Side" and contain no goodness at all. While for Jews, even their "Soul of Flesh and Blood" contains an element of good.

He lists five types of Jewish individuals according to their success in vanquishing their evil impulses:

1. The Complete Righteous
2. The Incomplete Righteous — who have not been completely successful
3. The Ordinary—who do the commandments but still have moments of evil thoughts
4. The Incomplete Wicked—who, while having good deeds to their credit, are still immersed in breaking the commandments and having evil thoughts
5. The Complete Wicked — whose existence is devoted to evil[16]

Zalman's son, Dov Baer (1773–1827), furthered his father's teachings in the brief *Tract on Ecstasy*.[17] His introduction posits a nullification of self through meditation that does not allow any thought to interfere with the complete unification with God.[18] What stands in the way of reaching this higher stage is the failure to achieve a broken heart that flows from the passion of true repentance.[19]

Dov Baer goes beyond the chauvinism of declaring Gentile souls to be on a lower level than Jewish souls. He asserted that the grouping of the Holy Sparks fell because of the "breaking of the vessels" among the idol worshippers for many hundreds of thousands of years. One can guess that few Gentiles would find this idea comforting! Gentiles who convert to Judaism reclaim these Holy Sparks.[20]

Another Hasidic *Admor* (master, rabbi, teacher) of increasing influence was Nahman of Bratslav (1772–1810). His mother, Feiga, was a daughter of Udel, who was the daughter of the Besht; his father, Simhah, was a son of Nahman of Horodenka, one of the Besht's students and a member of the first group of Hasidim. Nahman of Bratslav saw himself at a higher stage than the other tzaddikim and took no pains to conceal this opinion. His insistence on mystic devotion became the main aim of his movement. Every activity was to be directed toward achieving this. He laid great stress on communing with nature so as to lead to devotion to God. Nahman's Hasidim were bidden to follow his lead: seek meditation in seclusion and go into the fields to converse with God.

Nahman gained notoriety in the west as a consequence of his tales, which were popularized by Martin Buber in both German and English. The stories are on surprising topics such as those that tell of pirates and magic.

Nahman told his followers that they were to gather every Rosh HaShanah, even if doing so created great hardship. He also promised that, after his death, if one would come to his grave and follow a ritual prescribed by him, he personally would lift them up from the bottom of hell. Nahman had moved to Uman in th Ukraine because of his desire to associate himself with the martyrs of 1788 wh were buried there. Wracked by tuberculosis, Nahman continued his activities there even with great difficulty. He died during the holiday of Sukkot in 1810 and was buried in Uman. Nahman's scribe and promulgator of his thoughts, Rabbi Nathan Steinhartz (Reb Noson, 1780–1845), combined these two directives and instituted the annual pilgrimage to his grave there in Uman. Today thousands of Bratslaver Hasidim go on pilgrimage there. No tzadik succeeded Nahman as a leader of his group and so the Nahman's opponents refer to his group as the *Tote Hasidim* (dead Hasidim; they have no living leader).[21]

The rabbinical elite quite rightly assessed this threat to their dominance and, in the lands of Lithuania (including what is now Belarus), a movement gathered strength to combat it. The charges against the Hasidim were: their misconstruction of Lurianic Kabbalah regarding Tzimtzum (Shneur Zalman taught that the Tzimtzum only appeared to be real but was not actually so[22]); the popularization of Kabbalah, which was to be taught only to the worthy few; and the Hasidic doctrine of the tzadik. In biblical terms, a tzadik is a righteous human being.[23] According to Hasidism the tzadik is the charismatic man who is so elevated spiritually that those who follow him are elevated by osmosis. The eating of *shearayim* (remnant food) that the tzadik blessed and ate of is akin to the communion that is achieved by the imbibing of the Eucharist.

The most respected Talmudic authority of the day, Eliyah ben Shelomo Zalman (1720–1797), known as the Vilna Gaon (luminary, genius), was instrumental in excommunicating all who followed the Hasidic way.[24] But the excommunication was ineffective and withdrawn soon enough. The opponents of Hasidism are known as *Mitnagdim* (Opponents), their influence now shrunk to the walls of their yeshivot.

However, Mitnagdim and Hasidim were forced to join forces to combat the threats to Jewish orthodoxy that came from two directions. In Western Europe, an emancipated elite of sidelined rabbinical authority and wealthy lay leadership associated with secular organizations. In Eastern Europe, in the latter half of the nineteenth century, the socialist and Zionist movements became the dominant voices in community affairs, especially in metropolitan centers.

The Hasidic leaders were true to their love of their flocks and loyal enough to traditional Judaism not to stray from the precepts of the faith. In keeping with their understanding of the psychology of their followers, the Hasidic rebbes instituted even more severe prohibitions, as laxity in the performance of the commandments was looked upon as a sin.[25] Since the prophets, Judaism traditionally was given to the belief that if persecution or other disaster occurred, it had to be because of sin. Therefore the only way to avert or remedy disaster was to be even more punctilious n the performance of the commandments. The prohibition of secular studies not directly of use for religious study and the emphasis on separation by dress is directed to keep the adherents of Hasidism far from the temptations of the secular world.

On the last page of his monumental *Major Trends In Jewish Mysticism*, Gershom Scholem bemoans "the decay of a great movement."[26] He was referring to the loss of the original spiritual dynamism of Hasidism, the latest if not last manifestation of Jewish mysticism. In Hasidism, Kabbalah was popularized and went forth from the secret treasure of the few initiates to become the spiritual language of the masses. But what would Scholem say to the followers of Bratslav who chant and sticker "Na Nah Nahm Nahman mi-Uman" across the streets of Israel? To the many *ba'alei teshuvah* (penitents) and non-Hasidim who flock to Uman on Rosh HaShanah? Or to the emissaries of Chabad who, from the streets of Brooklyn to the Brandenburg Gate in Berlin, light giant hanukkiot?

Judaism never completely leaves the byways of its spiritual past. The Hekhalot hymns are present in the liturgy to this day. The meditation of Abulafia is revived in conjunction with the influence of the religions of the East. Hasidism attracts the most secular to its cause. The New Age mélange of ancient doctrine and modern thought is still developing. The new page in Jewish mysticism is being written as we write.

NOTES

1. See Simon M. Dubnow, *History of the Jews in Russia and Poland*, trans. I. Friedlander (New York: Ktav Publishing House, Inc., 1975), Vol. I.
2. See *Shulhan Arukh, Orah Hayyim* 94, notes of Rabbi Moses Isserles.
3. Most depictions of Jewish life in Eastern Europe tend to romanticize the conditions. For a sociological study see Mark Zborowski and Elizabeth Herzog, *Life Is with People* (New York: Schocken Books, 1962), Part II, "The Eastern Wall."
4. Dubnow, 220.
5. "Lilith (LXX. 'Ονοκένταυροι; Symmachus, Λάμια Vulg. 'Lamia')," *Jewish Encyclopedia,* http://www.jewishencyclopedia.com/articles/9986-lilith.
6. *Maggidim* were preachers who roamed the townlets of the Pale, preaching adherence to Jewish practice and ethics. They were not of the rabbinic intellectual class.
7. Dubnow, 225.
8. Ibid., 229–233.
9. Louis I. Newman and Samuel Spitz, *The Hasidic Anthology* (New York: Schocken Books, 1972). The source of this story is the book *Ozroth Idisher Humor* published by I. Ashkenazy in 1929.
10. Most Jews at the time would have some familiarity with the first *Ma'aseh* (story for legal and moral implication) found in the beginning of the Mishnah. Here Rabban Gamliel chides his sons for negligence in observing the commandment to say the morning declaration of faith. Mishnah Brakhot I:1.

11. One can experience this by going to a *tish* (lit. table, the gathering held by a Hasidic Rebbe or by viewing video recordings of these events (available on YouTube). When the late Lubavitche Rebbe Menahem Mendel Schneersohn was alive, he hosted *farbrengen* (Chabad gatherings) wher attendees would drink a *L'Hayyim* (toast "to life") to the Rebbe, hear his talk, and sing.

12. See Dubnow, 234, for a favorable view of Shneur Zalman.

13. "Shneor Zalman Ben Baruch (known also as Zalman Ladier)," *Jewish Encyclopedia*, http://www.jewishencyclopedia.com/articles/13599-shneor-zalman-ben-baruch.

14. Dubnow, 234, note 2.

15. See Simple explanations of the teachings of Shneur Zalman, Chabad.org, http://www.chabad.org/library/article_cdo/aid/2076435/jewish/Teachings.htm.

16. See *Tanya*, Intro. and Ch. 11, Chabad.org, http://www.chabad.org/library/tanya/tanya_cdo/aid/369735/jewish/page.htm.

17. Ibid., http://www.chabad.org/library/tanya/tanya_cdo/aid/1028862/jewish/Tanya.htm and *Kunteres HaHitpa'alut*, HebrewBooks.org, http://www.hebrewbooks.org/pdfpager.aspx?req=16042&st=&pgnum=39.

18. *Hakdamah MiKunteres HaHitpa'alut*, Chabad-Lubavitch Library, http://chabadlibrary.org/books/default.aspx?furl=/adhaam/maamarei/ku/3.

19. *Kunteres HaHitpa'alut*, Chabad-Lubavitch Library, http://chabadlibrary.org/books/default.aspx?furl=/adhaam/maamarei/ku/3.

20. Ibid.

21. "Nahman B. Simhah of Bratslav," *Jewish Encyclopedia*, http://www.jewishencyclopedia.com/articles/11282-nahman-b-simhah-of-bratzlav.

22. "Hasidim, Hasidism," *Jewish Encyclopedia*, http://www.jewishencyclopedia.com/articles/7317-hasidim-hasidism. See also Allan Nadler, *The Faith of the Mithnagdim* (Baltimore: Johns Hopkins University Press, 1997); Elijah Judah Schochet, *The Hasidic Movement and the Gaon of Vilna* (Northvale: J. Aronson, 1994); and Chabad.org, http://www.chabad.org/library/tanya/tanya_cdo/aid/369751/jewish/-.htm.

23. Gen. 18:23, where Abraham contrasts the Righteous and the Wicked; Prov. 13:5: "A Righteous man will hate a lie."

24. Dubnow, 235 f.

25. A visitor to the kosher section of any supermarket can readily see the increasing number of products that must bear the stamp of rabbinical supervision to allow their purchase by the religious consumer, even bottled water!

26. Scholem, *Major Trends*, 350.

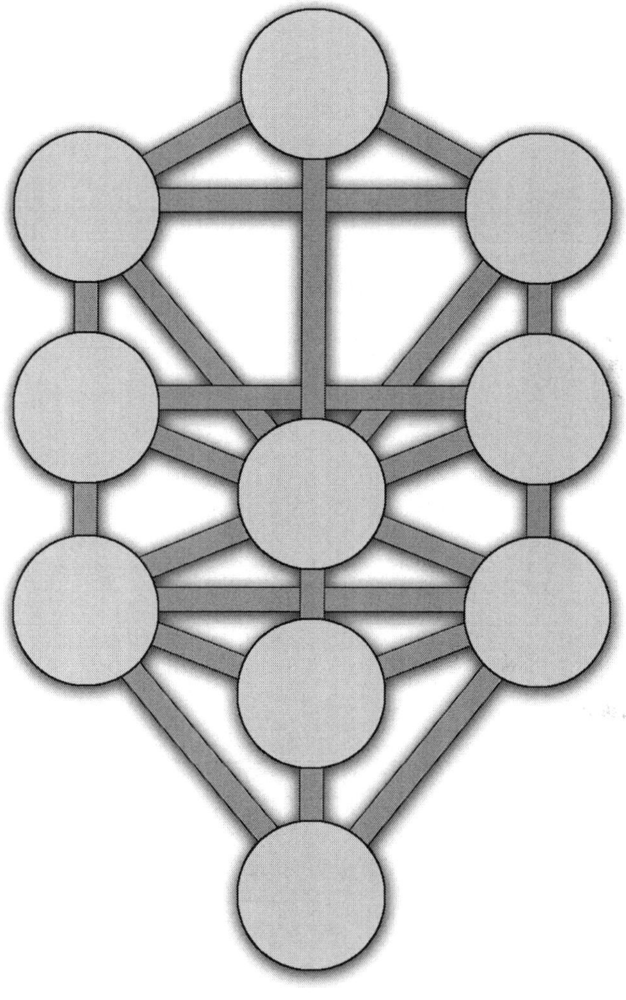

Afterword

But a guide to the Kabbalah would not be complete if it would be but an academic study.

Meditation, which has become so popular with the advent of the influence of Buddhism and Hinduism in the west, is an old practice of Kabbalah. As mentioned in the chapter on Abulafia, it was emphasized by him, if not one of his innovations. Believer or not, meditation on arising each morning before or in place of prayer is an excellent way to begin the day. Prayer and ritual are not favored among many moderns. But prayer and ritual are nothing more than bridges to spiritual experience. Bridges in themselves are not necessarily beautiful, but they are extremely useful if you wish to cross from one place to another. One of the failings of the non-Orthodox Jewish movements is the continuous production of new prayer books with translations that are interpretative and misleading, as the original text's real meaning may be somewhat embarrassing to the editors. English readings, responsive or otherwise, are interspersed in non-traditional services. This serves to break the tedium of a long service whose words in their original languages are unknown to the majority of would-be worshippers or, if known, without meaning especially to those not steeped in the tradition that brought them forth. But one who wishes to pray can find the original Hebrew and Aramaic to be most satisfying when said with fervor and intent. For the meaning of the recitation is the connection to generations past and the spirituality that was for them the reality of those words. We repeat their attempts, relying on their successful endeavors to be inspiring to us.

Anyone can attempt meditation. It is worth the effort to try the experience. For a simple method, sit on a comfortable seat on a straight-backed chair. Place your hands on your knees, hold your head high, and keep your eyes lowered. For a form of guided meditation, concentrate on the four Hebrew letters of the name of God. The technique of concentrating on one's out-breath can be used. One could imagine seeing the four letters of the Name disjointed into two sections of two letters each.

ה · ו   ה · י

The purpose is to see them separately and then, by your effort, to join them to complete the unification of the Name. That is similar to the kavanah of Lurianic

Kabbalah. We live in a disjointed world. This world needs tikkun. To meditat in such a manner, in place of or before prayer, begins the day with the purpose c charging oneself to make the world a better place by all of your acts. By observing o performing every mitzvah, we do bring about tikkun. For the spiritual path is th path that leads to peace and harmony. By following a spiritual path, the Jew is not only a monotheist but a monist to become one with the universe. Not to conquer nature but to be subsumed by it. Not oblivion but assimilation.

So be you believer or rational skeptic, you owe it to yourself to search out a community where the mystical elements of Judaism are still very much alive. Those who practice meditation know that attempts are met sometimes—many times—with failure, but perseverance is a necessity and the reward is too great to admit failure.

The next step is to participate in the observance of the Sabbath day. But short of that, find a service in your community for the closing services of Shabbat. Patiently peruse the prayer book as the afternoon service is recited. Wash your hands and partake of the hallah bread for that third meal (*seudat sh'lishit* or, in Yiddish, *shalisheudish*). Drink a *l'hayyim* (a toast to life) after the appropriate blessing. And hum if you cannot pronounce the words as the *zemirot* (hymns) are sung. You are now a courtier of the Palace of the King of Kings as the hymn of the AR"I B'nei Heikhalah is intoned.

> O courtiers of the palace, who yearn to see the splendor of Z'eir Anpin [The Impatient One]: Be present at this meal at which the King has engraved His signs. Be happy, rejoice in this gathering together with the angels and all heavenly beings; Rejoice now, at this most appropriate time, when there is no sadness.
>
> Draw near to Me, behold My strength, for there are no harsh judgments. They are cast out, they may not enter, these arrogant dogs [evil forces]. I invite the "Ancient of Days" at this auspicious time, and [all impure powers] will be surely removed.
>
> It is His revealed will to annul all the powers of impurity; He will hurl them into their abysses and He will hide them in the clefts of the rocks. For this time of Minhah [the afternoon prayer is the last Sabbath prayer] is a time of joy for Z'eir Anpin.

Grace after the meal is followed by evening prayer. The day is gone with havdalah, as the six-wicked candle is immersed in the wine after the blessing and the smelling of spices. As the smoke wafts upwards, nostalgia may grip you as you remember for a moment you were in the presence of the King. Is it an illusion or a super-reality?

But is Kabbalah and its purpose only for Jews? Perhaps the world is ready for Pan-Kabbalah!

Did not the prophet Malachi proclaim in the name of his God: "From sunrise to sunset my name is great among the nations. . . ." (Malachi 1:11)[1]

Rabbi Yehoshua ben Hananyah said: "All the righteous of the Gentiles have a share in the World to Come [Heaven].[2]

Rabbi Meir, a major contributor to the Mishnah, proclaimed: "A Gentile who studies Torah is like a High Priest" [and thus worthy to enter the Holy of Holies].[3]

The spiritual path is under attack from all sides. Beyond the attack of secularists who deny the existence of the spiritual, there is the failure of religious institutions. Too often the places to which we should turn for spiritual sustenance fail us because of charlatans who would manipulate the gullible.

There are too many leaders who betray their trust by the sexual and emotional abuse of those who entrust themselves to their care. Bureaucracy and emphasis on the mechanics of maintaining institutions stifle too many who are thirsty to drink from the well of spiritual strength. Dogmatic chauvinism and denial of the efficacy of separate spiritual paths turn off the innocent seeker at the first stop upon the path.

In each and every religious tradition we have:

1. The awe that we sense when we contemplate the mystery of creation and the majesty of our world.

2. The spiritual breakthrough whether it be the Buddha, Sinai, the Epiphany, or the voice that cried out to Muhammad, which in each instance created the great traditions of the past. Or the personal breakthrough that can happen to agnostics as they sense that there is more to be appreciated in this world than its mere materialistic aspect. Surely the words of Deuteronomy resound with all that wish to travel the spiritual path: " Man does not live by bread alone" (Deuteronomy 8:3).

3. The final purpose of our existence is a world where we can all live in peace with each other and do no harm to our wonderful biosphere.

All religions and spiritual quests are but spokes of the wheel. All the spokes lead to the center, where all coalesce in the peace of the Infinite that is beyond our immediate comprehension. The world needs spiritual activism to combat hatred, prejudice, cruelty and the abandonment of our less-fortunate brothers and sisters.

If each and every one of us could meditate in our own way every day on the reason for our existence, our place in the universe, and how we can contribute to that peace which is the sum of all visions of peace, then we can effect a true tikkun of our world.

A teacher can bring you to *A Gateway to the Kabbalah,* but you must push open the door to enter therein.

Great teachers such as Gershom Scholem and his students and those who have followed in his footsteps have explicated the Kabbalah as never has been done in past generations. Practioners such as Reb Zalman Schacter-Shelomi of blessed memory have inspired so many to follow the spiritual path.

Pope Francis has opened for his Church the envelope of Divine Compassion.

Madonna has popularized an interest in Kabbalah, proving that you do not have to be Jewish to follow this path. Her courage in exploring her spiritual dimensions is to be applauded.

In October 2014, high on the Himalayas after a treacherous sudden storm, German and Israeli trekkers found themselves facing hypothermia. Only by lying on top of one another could they maintain their own body heat and survive. What a powerful metaphor for all who seek spirituality. Only as we appreciate each other's path can we maintain in good faith our own!

Yes, great religions are like the spokes of a wheel, all directed to a center where peace and harmony reign. One should not abandon the traditions of one's youth because of the disillusionment that is so easy to come by and that is created by the moral and spiritual failings of leaders and practioners thereof. In each and every one of the great religious traditions there is a treasure trove to be mined for its spiritual insight. I who have meditated with a Karmapa, prayed in church and masjid, as well as having had the great good fortune to have been taught and sat at the feet of great rabbis know this to be a fact.

Will you find that spiritual experience?

Perhaps!

If you do not seek, you will not find.

If you seek, you will not find until you are found.

Robert Browning said in his poem, "Andrea del Sarto": "Ah, but a man's reach should exceed his grasp, Or what is a heaven for?"

NOTES

1. Malachi I:1
2. Tosefta Sanhedrin III:2
3. Bava Kama 38a. See also the Meiri to Bava Kama 38a, who states that Gentiles who follow religions that teach ethics are on equal footing with Jews.

Appendix

Books of the Zohar

1. The first book is an unnamed kabbalistic midrash on the entire Torah.
2. *Sifra diTseniuta* (Book of Concealment)
3. *Idra Rabba* (Great Assembly)
4. *Idra Zuta* (Lesser Assembly)
5. *Idra di-be-Mashkana* (Assembly dealing with the Tent [Tabernacle] in the Wilderness)
6. *Hekhalot* (Palaces [seven] seen by the soul after death)
7. *Raza de-Razin* (Secret of Secrets)
8. *Sava* (The Old Man)
9. *Yenuka* (The Child)
10. *Rav Metivata* (The Head of the Academy)
11. *Sitrei Torah* (Secrets of the Torah)
12. *Matnitin* (Mishnahs)
13. Zohar to the Song of Songs
14. *Kav Ha-Middah* (Mystical Standard of Measure)
15. *Sitrei Otiot* (Secret of the Letters)
16. This book is an unnamed commentary on Ezekiel's vision of the Merkabah (Chariot)
17. *Midrash Ha-Neelam* (Mystical Midrash on the Torah)
18. *Midrash Ha-Neelam* on the Book of Ruth (as above)
19. *Raya Mehemna* (The Faithful Shepherd)
20. *Tikkunei Zohar* (Emendations to the Zohar)

For a fuller description of these sections, see Gershom Scholem, *Major Trends in Jewish Mysticism* (New York: Schocken Books, 1974), 159–163.

For Further Reading

Abraham Abulafia

Idel, Moshe. *The Mystical Experience in Abraham Abulafia.* New York: SUNY Press, 1988.

Christian Cabala

Wirszubski, Chaim. *Pico della Mirandola's Encounter with Jewish Mysticism.* Cambridge: Harvard University Press, 1989.

Hasidism

Idel, Moshe. *Hasidism: Between Ecstasy and Magic.* New York: SUNY Press, 1995.

Wineberg, Rabbi Yosef. *Lessons in Tanya: The Tanya of R. Shneur Zalman of Liadi.* Volumes I–V. Brooklyn: Kehot Publication Society, 1998.

Kabbalah

Dan, Joseph. "Samael, Lilith, and the Concept of Evil in Early Kabbalah." Samuel, Gabriella. *The Kabbalah Handbook: A Concise Encyclopedia of Terms and Concepts in Jewish Mysticism.* New York: Penguin Books, 2007.

———, and R. Kiener. *The Early Kabbalah.* Mahwah, NJ: Paulist Press, 1986.

AJS Review, Volume V, 1980, 17–40.

Fine, Lawrence, ed. *Essential Papers in Kabbalah.* New York: NYU Press, 1995.

Green, Arthur. Ehyeh: A Kabbalah for Tomorrow. Woodstock, VT: Jewish Lights Publishing, 2003.

Hecker, Joel. *Mystical Bodies, Mystical Meals: Eating and Embodiment in Medieval Kabbalah.* Detroit: Wayne State University Press, 2005.

Idel, Moshe. *Kabbalah: New Perspectives.* New Haven: Yale University Press, 1988.

———. *Kabbalistic Prayer and Color: Approaches to Judaism in Medieval Times.* Edited by D. Blumenthal. Chicago: Scholar's Press, 1985.

———. *Magic and Kabbalah in the "Book of the Responding Entity."* The Solomon Goldman Lectures VI. Chicago: Spertus College of Judaica Press, 1993.

Scholem, Gershom. *Kabbalah.* Jewish Publication Society. Jerusalem: Jewish Publication Society, 1974.

Wolfson, Elliot. *Alef, Mem, Tau: Kabbalistic Musings on Time, Truth, and Death.* Berkeley: University of California Press, 2006.

———. *Language, Eros, Being: Kabbalistic Hermeneutics and Poetic Imagination.* New York: Fordham University Press, 2005.

———. *Venturing Beyond: Law and Morality in Kabbalistic Mysticism.* Oxford: Oxford University Press, 2006.

Mysticism

Dan, Joseph. *The Early Jewish Mysticism.* Tel Aviv: Mod Books, 1993.

———. *The Heart and the Fountain: An Anthology of Jewish Mystical Experiences.* New York: Oxford University Press, 2002.

———. *The "Unique Cherub" Circle: A School of Mystics and Esoterics in Medieval Germany.* Tübingen, Germany: J.C.B. Mohr, 1999.

Dennis, G. *The Encyclopedia of Jewish Myth, Magic, and Mysticism.* St. Paul, MN: Llewellyn Worldwide, 2007.

Fine, Lawrence, ed. *Judaism in Practice.* Princeton: Princeton University Press, 2001.

Grözinger, Karl E. *Jüdisches Denken: Theologie, Philosophie, Mystik. Band II, Von der mittelalterlichen Kabbala zum Hasidismus.* Frankfurt, Germany: Campus, 2005.

Idel, Moshe. *The Golem: Jewish Magical and Mystical Traditions on the Artificial Anthropoid.* New York: SUNY Press, 1990.

Scholem, Gershom. *Jewish Gnosticism, Merkabah Mysticism, and the Talmudic Tradition.* New York: The Jewish Theological Seminary, 1960.

———. *Major Trends in Jewish Mysticism.* New York: Schocken Books, 1941.

Wolfson, Elliot. *Through a Speculum That Shines: Vision and Imagination in Medieval Jewish Mysticism.* Princeton: Princeton University Press, 1994

Safed and Isaac Luria

Fine, Lawrence. *Physician of the Soul, Healer of the Cosmos: Isaac Luria and His Kabbalistic Fellowship.* Stanford: Stanford University Press, 2003.

———. *Safed Spirituality.* Mahwah, NJ: Paulist Press, 1989.

Idel, Moshe. "The Story of Rabbi Joseph della Reina." Behayahu, M. *Studies and Texts on the History of the Jewish Community in Safed.* New York: Judaica Press, 1993.

Scholem, Gershom. *Sabbatai Sevi: The Mystical Messiah.* Translated by R. J. Zwi Werblowsky. Bollingen Series XCIII. Princeton: Princeton University Press, 1973.

Zohar

Scholem, Gershom, and Melila Hellner-Eshed. "Zohar." *Encyclopaedia Judaica,* Second Edition. Edited by Michael Berenbaum and Fred Skolnik. Volume XXI. Detroit: Macmillan Reference USA, 2007, 647–64. Gale Virtual Reference Library.

Tishby, Isaiah, ed. *The Wisdom of the Zohar: An Anthology of Texts.* Volumes I–III. Translated by David Goldstein. Oxford: The Littman Library of Jewish Civilization, 1989.

Wolfson, Elliot. *Luminal Darkness: Imaginal Gleanings from Zoharic Literature.* London: Oneworld Publications, 2006.

Bibliography

Alon, Gedalyahu. *The Jews in Their Land*. Cambridge: Harvard University Press, 1980.

Anderson, Bernhard W. *Understanding the Old Testament*. Upper Saddle River. NJ: Prentice Hall, 1986.

Baron, Salo Wittmayer. *A Social and Religious History of the Jews*. Volume III. New York: Columbia University Press, 1969.

Brown, Louise Fargo. *The Political Activities of the Baptists and the Fifth Monarchy Men in England During the Interregnum*. London: Oxford University Press, 1912.

Cohen, Boaz. *Jewish and Roman Law: A Comparative Study in Two Volumes*. New York: The Jewish Theological Seminary, 2012.

Dubnow, Simon M. *History of the Jews in Russia and Poland*. Translated by I. Friedlander. New York: Ktav Publishing House, 1975.

Eissfeldt, Otto. *The Old Testament*. Translated by Peter R. Ackroyd. New York and Evanston: Harpers and Row Publishers, 1966.

Finkelstein, Louis. *Akiva: Scholar, Saint and Martyr*. New York: Atheneum, 1970.

Ginsberg, H. Louis. *Studies in Daniel*. New York: The Jewish Theological Seminary, 1948.

Goodenough, Erwin Ramsdell. *Jewish Symbols in the Greco-Roman Period*. Bollingen Series XXXVII. Princeton: Princeton University Press, 1953.

Graetz, Heinrich. *History of the Jews*. Philadelphia: Jewish Publication Society, 1956.

Guthrie, William Keith Chambers. *Orpheus and Greek Religion: A Study of the Orphic Movement*. Princeton: Princeton University Press, 1952.

Harnack, Adolph. *History of Dogma, Volume IV*. Translated by Neil Buchanan. New York: Dover Publications, 1961.

Idel, Moshe. *The Mystical Experience in Abraham Abulafia*. Albany: SUNY Press, 1947.

Kamenetz, Rodger. *The Jew in the Lotus.* San Francisco: Harper One, 1995.

Newman, Louis I., with Samuel Spitz. *The Hasidic Anthology.* New York: Schocken Books, 1972, with stories originally published in *Ozroth Idisher Humor.* New York: I. Ashkenazy, 1929.

Kramer, Samuel Noah. *History Begins at Sumer.* Philadelphia: University of Pennsylvania Press, 1973.

Meier, John P. *A Marginal Jew: Rethinking the Historical Jesus.* Volumes I–IV. The Anchor Yale Bible Reference Library. New Haven: Yale University Press, 1991–2009.

Roth, Cecil. *The Jews in the Renaissance.* Philadelphia: Jewish Publication Society, 1978.

Scholem, Gershom. *Jewish Gnosticism, Merkabah Mysticism, and the Talmudic Tradition.* New York: The Jewish Theological Seminary, 1960.

———. *Major Trends in Jewish Mysticism.* New York: Schocken Books, 1974.

———. *Sabbatai Sevi: The Mystical Messiah.* Translated by R. J. Zwi Werblowsky. Bollingen Series XCIII. Princeton: Princeton University Press, 1973.

Steinsaltz, Adin. *The Thirteen Petalled Rose.* New York: Basic Books, 1980.

Urbach, Ephraim E. *The Sages.* Translated by Israel Abrahams. Cambridge: Harvard University Press, 1987.

Werblowsky, R. J. Zwi. *Joseph Karo: Lawyer and Mystic.* Philadelphia: The Jewish Publication Society, 1977.

West, Martin. *The East Face of Helicon: West Asiatic Elements in Greek Poetry and Myth.* London: Oxford University Press, 1997.

Zborowski, Mark, and Elizabeth Herzog. *Life Is with People: The Culture of the Shtetl.* New York: Schocken Books, 1962.